ENGLISH HOUSEWIFERY EXEMPLIFIED IN ABOVE FOUR HUNDRED AND FIFTY RECEIPTS GIVING DIRECTIONS FOR MOST PARTS OF COOKERY • MOXON, ELIZABETH

Publisher's Note

Purchase of this book entitles you to a free trial membership in the publisher's book club at www.rarebooksclub.com. (Time limited offer.) Simply enter the barcode number from the back cover onto the membership form on our home page. The book club entitles you to select from millions of books at no additional charge. You can also download a digital copy of this and related books to read on the go. Simply enter the title or subject onto the search form to find them.

Note: This is an historic book. Pages numbers, where present in the text, refer to the first edition of the book and may also be in indexes.

If you have any questions, could you please be so kind as to consult our Frequently Asked Questions page at www.rarebooksclub.com/faqs.cfm? You are also welcome to contact us there.

Publisher: General Books LLC™, Memphis, TN, USA, 2012. ISBN: 9781153604345.

Proofreading: pgdp.net

⁂ ⁂ ⁂ ⁂ ⁂ ⁂ ⁂ ⁂

ENGLISH HOUSEWIFRY

EXEMPLIFIED

In above FOUR HUNDRED AND FIFTY RECEIPTS,
Giving DIRECTIONS in most PARTS of COOKERY;
And how to prepare various SORTS of
  SOOPS, CAKES,
  MADE-DISHES, CREAMS,
  PASTES, JELLIES,
  PICKLES, MADE-WINES, &c.
With CUTS for the orderly placing the DISHES and COURSES; also Bills of Fare for every Month in the Year; and an alphabetical INDEX to the Whole.

A BOOK necessary for Mistresses of Families, higher and lower Women Servants, and confined to Things USEFUL, SUBSTANTIAL and SPLENDID, and calculated for the Preservation of HEALTH, and upon the Measures of *Frugality*, being the Result of thirty Years *Practice* and *Experience*.

By ELIZABETH MOXON.

WITH An APPENDIX CONTAINING, Upwards of Sixty RECEIPTS, of the most valuable Kind, communicated to the Publisher by several Gentlewomen in the Neighbourhood, distinguished by their extraordinary Skill in HOUSEWIFRY.

THE RETURNS OF SPIRITUAL COMFORT and GRIEF, In a Devout SOUL.

Represented by an Intercourse of Letters to the Right Honourable Lady LETICE, Countess of Falkland, in her Life Time.

Publish'd for the Benefit and Ease of all who labour under Spiritual Afflictions.

1764.

THE PREFACE

It is not doubted but the candid Reader will find the following BOOK in correspondence with the title, which will supersede the necessity of any other recommendation that might be given it.

As the complier of it engaged in the undertaking at the instance and importunity of many persons of eminent account and distinction, so she can truly assure them, and the world, that she has acquitted herself with the utmost care and fidelity.

And she entertains the greater hopes that her performance will meet with the kinder acceptance, because of the good opinion she has been held in by those, her ever honour'd friends, who first excited her to the publication of her BOOK, and who have been long eye-witnesses of her skill and behaviour in the business of her calling.

She has nothing to add, but her humblest thanks to them, and to all others with whom she has received favour and encouragement.

ENGLISH HOUSEWIFRY.

1. *To make* VERMICELLY SOOP.

Take a neck of beef, or any other piece; cut off some slices, and fry them with butter 'till they are very brown; wash your pan out every time with a little of the gravy; you may broil a few slices of the beef upon a grid-iron: put all together into a pot, with a large onion, a little salt, and a little whole pepper; let it stew 'till the meat is tender, and skim off the fat in the boiling; them strain it into your dish, and boil four ounces of vermicelly in a little of the gravy 'till it is soft: Add a little stew'd spinage; then put all together into a dish, with toasts of bread; laying a little vermicelly upon the toast. Garnish your dish with creed rice and boil'd spinage, or carrots slic'd thin.

2. **CUCUMBER SOOP.**

Take a houghil of beef, break it small and put it into a stew-pan, with part of a neck of mutton, a little whole pepper, an onion, and a little salt; cover it with water, and let it stand in the oven all night, then strain it and take off the fat; pare six or eight middle-siz'd cucumbers, and slice them not very thin, stew them in a little butter and a little whole pepper; take them out of the butter and put 'em in the gravy. Garnish your dish with raspings of bread, and serve it up with toasts of bread or *French* roll.

3. *To make* HARE SOOP.

Cut the hare into small pieces, wash it and put it into a stew-pan, with a knuckle of veal; put in it a gallon of water, a little salt, and a handful of sweet herbs; let it stew 'till the gravy be good; fry a little of the hare to brown the soop; you may put in it some crusts of write bread among the meat to thicken the soop; put it into a dish, with a little stew'd spinage, crisp'd bread, and a few forc'd-meat balls. Garnish your dish with boil'd spinage and turnips, cut it in thin square slices.

4. *To make Green* PEASE SOOP.

Take a neck of mutton, and a knuckle of veal, make of them a little good gravy; then take half a peck of the greenest young peas, boil and beat them to a pulp in a marble mortar; then put to them a little of the gravy; strain them through a hair sieve to take out all the pulp; put all together, with a little salt and whole pepper; then boil it a little, and if you think the soop not green enough, boil a handful of spinage very tender, rub it through a hair-sieve, and put into the soop with one spoonful of wheat-flour, to keep it from running: You must not let it boil after the spinage is put in, it will discolour it; then cut white bread in little diamonds, fry them in butter while crisp, and put it into a dish, with a few whole peas. Garnish your dish with creed rice, and red beet-root.

You may make asparagus-soop the same way, only add tops of asparagus, instead of whole pease.

5. *To make* ONION SOOP.

Take four or five large onions, pill and boil them in milk and water whilst tender, (shifting them two or three times in the boiling) beat 'em in a marble mortar to a pulp, and rub them thro' a hair-sieve, and put them into a little sweet gravy; then fry a few slices of veal, and two or three slices of lean bacon; beat them in a marble mortar as small as forc'd-meat; put it into your stew-pan with the gravy and onions, and boil them; mix a spoonful of wheat-flour with a little water, and put it into the soop to keep it from running; strain all through a cullender, season it to your taste; then put into the dish a little spinage stew'd in butter, and a little crisp bread; so serve it up.

6. *Common* PEASE SOOP *in Winter.*

Take a quart of good boiling pease which put into a pot with a gallon of soft water whilst cold; add thereto a little beef or mutton, a little hung beef or bacon, and two or three large onions; boil all together while your soop is thick; salt it to your taste, and thicken it with a little wheat-flour; strain it thro' a cullender, boil a little sellery, cut it in small pieces, with a little crisp bread, and crisp a little spinage, as you would do parsley, then put it in a dish, and serve it up. Garnish your dish with raspings of bread.

7. *To make* PEASE SOOP *in Lent.*

Take a quart of pease, put them into a pot with a gallon of water, two or three large onions, half a dozen anchovies, a little whole pepper and salt; boil all together whilst your soop is thick; strain it into a stew-pan through a cullender, and put six ounces of butter (work'd in flour) into the soop to thicken it; also put in a little boil'd sellery, stew'd spinage, crisp bread, and a little dry'd mint powdered; so serve it up.

8. CRAW-FISH SOOP.

Take a knuckle of veal, and part of a neck of mutton to make white gravy, putting in an onion, a little whole pepper and salt to your taste; then take twenty crawfish, boil and beat them in a marble mortar, adding thereto alittle of the gravy; strain them and put them into the gravy; also two or three pieces of white bread to thicken the soop; boil twelve or fourteen of the smallest crawfish, and put them whole into the dish, with a few toasts, or *French* roll, which you please; so serve it up.

You may make lobster soop the same way, only add into the soop the seeds of the lobster.

9. *To make* SCOTCH SOOP.

Take a houghil of beef, cut it in pieces, with part of a neck of mutton, and a pound of *French* barley; put them all into your pot, with six quarts of water; let it boil 'till the barley be soft, then put in a fowl; as soon as 'tis enough put in a handful of red beet leaves or brocoli, a handful of the blades of onions, a handful of spinage, washed and shred very small; only let them have a little boil, else it will spoil the greenness. Serve it up with the fowl in a dish, garnish'd with raspings of bread.

10. *To make* SOOP *without Water.*

Take a small leg of mutton, cut it in slices, season it with a little pepper and salt; cut three middling turnips in round pieces, and three small carrots scrap'd and cut in pieces, a handful of spinage, a little parsley, a bunch of sweet herbs, and two or three cabbage lettice; cut the herbs pretty small, lay a row of meat and a row of herbs; put the turnips and carrots at the bottom of the pot, with an onion, lay at the top half a pound of sweet butter, and close up the pot with coarse paste; them put the pot into boiling water, and let it boil for four hours; or in a slow oven, and let it stand all night; when it is enough drain the gravy from the meat, skim off the fat, then put it into your dish with some toasts of bread, and a little stew'd spinage; to serve it up.

11. *To stew a* BRISKET *of* BEEF.

Take the thin part of a brisket of beef, score the skin at the top; cross and take off the under skin, then take out the bones, season it highly with mace, a little salt, and a little whole pepper, rub it on both sides, let it lay all night, make broth of the bones, skim the fat clean off, put in as much water as will cover it well, let it stew over a slow fire four or five hours, with a bunch of sweet herbs and an onion cut in quarters; turn the beef over every hour, and when you find it tender take it out of the broth and drain it very well, having made a little good strong gravy.

A ragoo with sweet-breads cut into pieces, pullets tenderly boil'd and cut in long pieces; take truffles and morels, if you have any mushrooms, with a little claret, and throw in your beef, let it stew a quarter of an hour in the ragoo, turning it over sometimes, then take out your beef, and thicken your ragoo with a lump of butter and a little flour. Garnish your dish with horse-radish and pickles, lay the ragoo round your beef, and a little upon the top; so serve it up.

12. *To stew a* RUMP *of* BEEF.

Take a fat rump of young beef and cut off the fag end, lard the low part with fat bacon, and stuff the other part with shred parsley; put it into your pan with two or three quarts of water, a quart of Claret, two or three anchovies, an onion, two or three blades of mace, a little whole pepper, and a bunch of sweet herbs; stew it over a slow fire five or six hours, turning it several times in the stewing, and keep it close cover'd; when your beef is enough take from it the gravy, thicken part of it with a lump of butter and flour, and put it upon the dish with the beef. Garnish the dish with horse-radish and red-beet root. There must be no salt upon the beef, only salt the gravy to your taste.

You may stew part of a brisket, or an ox cheek the same way.

13. *To make* OLIVES *of* BEEF.

Take some slices of a rump (or any other tender piece) of beef, and beat them with a paste pin, season them with nutmeg, pepper and salt, and rub them over with the yolk of an egg; make a little forc'd-meat of veal, beef-suet, a few bread crumbs, sweet-herbs, a little shred mace, pepper, salt, and two eggs, mixed all together; take two or three slices of the beef, according as they are in bigness, and a lump of forc'd-meat the size of an egg; lay your beef round it, and roll it in part of a kell of veal, put it into an earthen dish, with a little water, a glass of claret, and a little onion shred small; lay upon them a little butter, and bake them in an oven about an hour; when they come out take off the fat, and thicken the gravy with a little butter and flour; six of them is enough for a side dish. Garnish the dish with horseradish and pickles.

You may make olives of veal the same way.

14. *To fry* BEEF-STEAKS.

Take your beef steaks and beat them with the back of a knife, fry them in butter over a quick fire, that they may be brown before they be too much done; when they are enough put them into an earthen pot whilst you have fry'd them all; pour out the fat, and put them into your pan with a little gravy, an onion shred very small, a spoonful of catchup and a little salt; thicken it with a little butter and flour, the thickness of cream.

Garnish your dish with pickles.

Beef-steaks are proper for a side-dish.

15. BEEF-STEAKS *another Way*.

Take your beef-steaks and beat them with the back of a knife, strow them over with a little pepper and salt, lay them on a grid-iron over a clear fire, turning 'em whilst enough; set your dish over a chafing-dish of coals, with a little brown gravy; chop an onion or Shalot as small as pulp, and put it amongst the gravy; (if your steaks be not over much done, gravy will come therefrom;) put it on a dish and shake it all together. Garnish your dish with shalots and pickles.

16. *A* SHOULDER *of* MUTTON *forc'd*.

Take a pint of oysters and chop them, put in a few bread-crumbs, a little pepper, shred mace, and an onion, mix them all together, and stuff your mutton on both sides, then roast it at a slow fire, and baste it with nothing but butter; put into the dripping-pan a little water, two or three spoonfuls of the pickle of oysters, a glass of claret, an onion shred small, and an anchovy; if your liquor waste before your mutton is enough, put in a little more water; when the meat is enough, take up the gravy, skim off the fat, and thicken it with flour and butter; then serve it up. Garnish your dish with horse-radish and pickles.

17. *To stew a* FILLET *of* MUTTON.

Take a fillet of mutton, stuff it the same as for a shoulder, half roast it, and put it into a stew pan with a little gravy, a jill of claret, an anchovy, and a shred onion; you may put in a little horse-radish and some mushrooms; stew it over a slow fire while the mutton is enough; take the gravy, skim off the fat, and thicken it with flour and butter; lay forc'd-meat-balls round the mutton. Garnish your dish with horse-radish and mushrooms.

It is proper either for a side-dish or bottom dish; if you have it for a bottom-dish, cut your mutton into two fillets.

18. *To Collar a Breast of* MUTTON.

Take a breast of mutton, bone it, and season it with nutmeg, pepper and salt, rub it over with the yolk of an egg; make a little forc'd-meat of veal or mutton, chop it with a little beef-suet, a few bread-crumbs, sweet herbs, an onion, pepper and salt, a little nutmeg, two eggs, and a spoonful or two of cream; mix all together and lay it over the mutton, roll it up and bind it about with course inkle; put it into an earthen dish with a little water, dridge it over with flour, and lay upon it a little butter; it will require two hours to bake it. When it is enough take up the gravy, skim off the fat, put in an anchovy and a spoonful of catchup, thicken it with flour and butter; take the inkle from the mutton and cut it into three or four rolls; pour the sauce upon the dish, and lay about it forc'd-meat-balls. Garnish your dish with pickles.

19. *To Collar a Breast of* MUTTON *another Way*.

Take a breast of mutton, bone it, and season it with nutmeg, pepper and salt; roll it up tight with coarse incle and roast it upon a spit; when it is enough lay it whole upon the dish. Then take four or six cucumbers, pare them and cut them in slices, not very thin; likewise cut three or four in quarters length way, stew them in a little brown gravy and a little whole pepper; when they are enough thicken them with flour and butter the thickness of cream; so serve it up. Garnish your dish with horse-radish.

20. *To Carbonade a Breast of* MUTTON.

Take a breast of mutton, half bone it, nick it cross, season it with pepper and salt; then broil it before the fire whilst it be enough, strinkling it over with bread-crumbs; let the sauce be a little gravy and butter, and a few shred capers; put it upon the dish with the mutton. Garnish it with horse-radish and pickles.

This is proper for a side-dish at noon, or a bottom-dish at night.

21. *A Chine of* MUTTON *roasted, with stew'd* SELLERY.

Take a loyn of mutton, cut off the thin part and both ends, take off the skin, and score it in the roasting as you would do pork; then take a little sellery, boil it, and cut it in pieces about an inch long, put to it a little good gravy, while pepper and salt, two or three spoonfuls of cream and a lump of butter, so thicken it up, and pour it upon your dish with your mutton.—This is proper for a side-dish.

22. MUTTON-CHOPS.

Take a leg of mutton half-roasted, when it is cold cut it in thin pieces as you would do any other meat for hashing, put it into a stew-pan with a little water or small gravy, two or three spoonfuls of claret, two or three shalots shred, or onions, and two or three spoonfuls of oyster pickle; thicken it up with a little flour, and so serve it up. Garnish your dish with horse-radish and pickles.

You may do a shoulder of mutton the same way, only boil the blade-bone, and lie in the middle.

23. *A forc'd* LEG *of* MUTTON.

Take a leg of mutton, loose the skin from the meat, be careful you do not cut the skin as you loosen it; then cut the meat from the bone, and let the bone and skin hang together, chop the meat small, with a little beef-suet, as you would do sausages; season it with nutmeg, pepper and salt, a few bread-crumbs, two or three eggs, a little dry'd sage, shred parsley and lemon-peel; then fill up the skin with forc'd-meat, and lay it upon an earthen dish; lay upon the meat a little flour and butter, and a little water in the dish; it will take an hour and a half baking; when you dish it up lay about it either mutton or veal chollops, with brown gravy sauce. Garnish your dish with horse-radish and lemon. You may make a forc'd leg of lamb the same way.

24. *To make* FRENCH CUTLETS *of* MUTTON.

Take a neck of mutton, cut it in joints, cut off the ends of the long bones, then scrape the meat clean off the bones about an inch, take a little of the inpart of the meat of the cutlets, and make it into forc'd-meat; season it with nutmeg, pepper, and salt; then lay it upon your cutlets, rub over them the yolk of an egg to make it stick; chop a few sweet herbs, and put to them a few bread-crumbs, a little pepper and salt, and strew it over the cutlets, and wrap them in double writing-paper; either broil them before the fire or in an oven, half an hour will do them; when you dish them up, take off the out-paper, and set in the midst of the dish a little brown gravy in a china-bason; you may broil them without paper if you please.

25. *To fry* MUTTON STEAKS.

Take a loyn of mutton, cut off the thin part, then cut the rest into steaks, and flat them with a bill, season them with a little pepper and salt, fry them in butter over a quick fire; as you fry them put them into a stew-pan or earthen-pot, whilst you have fried them all; then pour the fat out of the pan, put in a little gravy, and the gravy that comes from the steaks, with a spoonful of claret, an anchovy, and an onion or a shalot shred; shake up the steaks in the gravy, and thicken it with a little flour; so serve them up. Garnish your dish with horse radish and shalots.

26. *To make artificial* VENISON *of* MUTTON.

Take a large shoulder of mutton, or a middling fore quarter, bone it, lay it in an earthen dish, put upon it a pint of claret, and let it lie all night; when you put it into your pasty-pan or dish, pour on the claret that it lay in, with a little water and butter; before you put it into your pasty-pan, season it with pepper and salt; when you make the pasty lie no paste in the bottom of the dish.

27. *How to brown Ragoo a* BREAST *of* VEAL.

Take a breast of veal, cut off both the ends, and half roast it; then put it into a stew-pan, with a quart of brown gravy, a spoonful of mushroom-powder, a blade or two of mace, and lemon-peel; so let it stew over a slow fire whilst your veal is enough; then put in two or three shred mushrooms or oysters, two or three spoonfuls of white wine; thicken up your sauce with flour and butter; you may lay round your veal some stew'd morels and truffles; if you have none, some pallets stew'd in gravy, with artichoke-bottoms cut in quarters, dipt in eggs and fry'd, and some forc'd-meat-balls; you may fry the sweet-bread cut in pieces, and lay over the veal, or fry'd oysters; when you fry your oysters you must dip them in egg and flour mixed. Garnish your dish with lemon and pickles.

28. *A Herico of a* BREAST *of* VEAL, *French Way.*

Take a breast of veal, half roast it, then put it into a stew-pan, with three pints of brown gravy; season your veal with nutmeg, pepper and salt; when your veal is stew'd enough, you may put in a pint of green peas boil'd. Take six middling cucumbers, pare and cut them in quarters long way, also two cabbage-lettices, and stew them in brown gravy; so lay them round your veal when you dish it up, with a few forc'd-meat-balls and some slices of bacon. Garnish your dish with pickles, mushrooms, oysters and lemons.

29. *To roll a* BREAST *of* VEAL.

Take a breast of veal, and bone it, season it with nutmeg, pepper and salt, rub it over with the yolk of an egg, and strew it over with sweet herbs shred small, and some slices of bacon, cut thin to lie upon it, roll it up very tight, bind it with coarse inkle, put it into an earthen dish with a little water, and lay it upon some lumps of butter; strew a little seasoning on the outside of your veal, it will take two hours baking; when it is baked take off the inkle and cut it in four rolls, lay it upon the dish with a good brown gravy-sauce: lay about your veal the sweet-bread fry'd, some forc'd-meat-balls, a little crisp bacon, and a few fry'd oysters if you have any; so serve it up. Garnish your dish with pickles and lemon.

30. *A stew'd* BREAST *of* VEAL.

Take the fattest and whitest breast of veal you can get, cut off both ends and boil them for a little gravy; take the veal and raise up the thin part, make a forc'd-meat of the sweet-bread boil'd, a few bread-crumbs, a little beef-suet, two eggs, pepper and salt, a spoonful or two of cream, and a little nutmeg, mix'd all together; so stuff the veal, skewer the skin close down, dridge it over with flour, tie it up in a cloth, and boil it in milk and water about an hour. For the sauce take a little gravy, about a jill of oysters, a few mushrooms shred, a little lemon shred fine, and a little juice of lemon; so thicken it up with flour and butter; when you dish it up pour the same over it; lay over it a sweet-bread or two cut in slices and fry'd, and fry'd oysters. Garnish your dish with lemon, pickles and mushrooms.

This is proper for a top dish either at noon or night.

31. *To stew a* FILLET *of* VEAL.

Take a leg of the best whye veal, cut off the dug and the knuckle, cut the rest into two fillets, and take the fat part and cut it in pieces the thickness of your finger; you must stuff the veal with the fat; make the hole with a penknife, draw it thro' and skewer it round; season it with pepper, salt, nutmeg, and shred parsley; then put it into your stew-pan, with half a pound of butter, (without water) and set it on your stove; let it boil very slow and cover it close up, turning it very often; it will take about two hours in stewing; when it is enough pour the gravy from it, take off the fat, put into the gravy a pint of oysters and a few capers, a little lemon-peel, a spoonful or two of white wine, and a little juice of lemon; thicken it with butter and flour the thickness of cream; lay round it forc'd-meat-balls and oysters fry'd, and so serve it up. Garnish your dish with a few capers and slic'd lemon.

32. *To make* SCOTCH COLLOPS.

Take a leg of veal, take off the thick part and cut in thin slices for collops, beat them with a paste-pin 'till they be very thin; season them with mace, pepper and salt; fry them over a quick fire, not over brown; when they are fried put them into a stew-pan with a little gravy, two or three spoonfuls of white wine, two spoonfuls of oyster-pickle if you have it, and a little lemon-peel; then shake them over a stove in a stew-pan, but don't let them boil over much, it only hardens your collops; take the fat part of your veal, stuff it with forc'd-meat, and boil it; when it is boiled lay it in the middle of your dish with the collops; lay about your collops slices of crisp bacon, and forc'd-meat-balls. Garnish your dish with slices of lemon and oysters, or mushrooms.

33. *To make* VEAL CUTLETS.

Take a neck of veal, cut it in joints, and flatten them with a bill; cut off the ends of the bones, and lard the thick part of the cutlets with four or five bits of bacon; season it with nutmeg pepper and salt; strew over them a few bread crumbs, and sweet herbs shred fine; first dip the cutlets in egg to make the crumbs stick, then broil them before the fire, put to them a little brown gravy sauce, so serve it up. Garnish your dish with lemon.

34. VEAL CUTLETS *another Way*.

Take a neck of veal, cut it in joints, and flat them as before, and cut off the ends of the long bones; season them with a little pepper, salt and nutmeg, broil them on a gridiron, over a slow fire; when they are enough, serve them up with brown gravy sauce and forc'd-meat-balls. Garnish your dish with lemon.

35. VEAL CUTLETS *another Way*.

Take a neck of veal and cut it in slices, flatten them as before, and cut off the ends of the long bones; season the cutlets with pepper and salt, and dridge over them some flour; fry them in butter over a quick fire; when they are enough put from them the fat they were fried in, and put to them a little small gravy, a spoonful of catchup, a spoonful of white wine or juice of lemon, and grate in some nutmeg; thicken them with flour and butter, so serve them up. Garnish your dish as before.

36. *To Collar a* CALF'S HEAD *to eat hot*.

Take a large fat head, and lay it in water to take out the blood; boil it whilst the bones will come out; season it with nutmeg, pepper and salt; then wrap it up round with a large lump of forc'd-meat made of veal; after which wrap it up tight in a veal kell before it is cold, and take great care that you don't let the head break in two pieces; then bind it up with a coarse inkle, lay it upon an earthen dish, dridge it over with flour, and lay over it a little butter, with a little water in the dish; an hour and a half will bake it; when it is enough take off the inkle, cut it in two length ways, laying the skin-side uppermost; when you lay it upon your dish you must lay round it stew'd pallets and artichoke-bottoms fry'd with forc'd-meat-balls; put to it brown gravy-sauce; you may brown your sauce with a few truffles or morels, and lay them about your veal.

Garnish your dish with lemon and pickle.

37. *To Collar a* CALF'S HEAD *to eat cold*.

You must be a calf's head with the skin on, split it and lay it in water, take out the tongue and eyes, cut off the groin ends, then tie it up in a cloth and boil it whilst the bones come out; when it is enough lay it on a table with the skin-side uppermost, and pour upon it a little cold water; then take off the hair and cut off the ears; mind you do not break the head in two, turn it over and take out the bones; salt it very well and wrap it round in a cloth very tight, pin it with pins, and tie it at both ends, so bind it up with broad inkle, then hang it up by one end, and when it is cold take it out; you must make for it brown pickle, and it will keep half a year; when you cut it, cut it at the neck.

It is proper for a side or middle dish, either for noon or night.

38. *To make a* CALF'S HEAD *Hash*.

Take a calf's head and boil it, when it is cold take one half of the head and cut off the meat in thin slices, put it into a stew pan with a little brown gravy, put to it a spoonful or two of walnut pickle, a spoonful of catchup, a little claret, a little shred mace, a few capers shred, or a little mango; boil it over a stove, and thicken it with butter and flour; take the other part of the head, cut off the bone ends and score it with a knife, season it with a little pepper and salt, rub it over with the yolk of an egg, and strew over a few bread crumbs, and a little parsley; then set it before the fire to broil whilst it is brown; and when you dish up the other part lay this in the midst; lay about your hash-brain-cakes, forc'd-meat-balls and crisp bacon.

To make Brain-cakes; take a handful of bread-crumbs, a little shred lemon-peel, pepper, salt, nutmeg, sweet-marjorum, parsley shred fine, and the yolks of three eggs; take the brains and skin them, boil and chop them small, so mix them all together; take a little butter in your pan when you fry them, and drop them in as you do fritters, and if they run in your pan put in a handful more of bread-crumbs.

39. *To hash a* CALF'S HEAD *white.*

Take a calf's head and boil it as much as you would do for eating, when it is cold cut in thin slices, and put it into a stew-pan with a white gravy; then put to it a little shred mace, salt, a pint of oysters, a few shred mushrooms, lemon-peel, three spoonful of white wine, and some juice of lemon, shake all together, and boil it over the stove, thicken it up with a little flour and butter; when you put it on your dish, you must put a boil'd fowl in the midst, and few slices of crisp bacon.

Garnish your dish with pickles and lemon.

40. *A Ragoo of a* CALF'S HEAD.

Take two calves' head and boil them as you do for eating, when they are cold cut off all the lantern part from the flesh in pieces about an inch long, and about the breadth of your little finger; put it into your stew-pan with a little white gravy; twenty oysters cut in two or three pieces, a few shred mushrooms, and a little juice of lemon; season it with shred mace and salt, let them all boil together over a stove; take two or three spoonfuls of cream, the yolks of two or three eggs, and a little shred parsley, then put it into a stew-pan; after you have put the cream in you may shake it all the while; if you let it boil it will crudle, so serve it up.

Garnish your dish with sippets, lemon, and a few pickled mushrooms.

41. *To roast a* CALF'S HEAD *to eat like Pig.*

Take a calf's head, wash it well, lay it in an earthen dish, and cut out the tongue lay it loose under the head in the dish with the brains, and a little sage and parsley; rub the head over with the yolk of an egg, then strew over them a few bread-crumbs and shred parsley, lay all over it lumps of butter and a little salt, then set it in the oven; it will take about an hour and a half baking; when it is enough take the brains, sage and parsley; and chop them together, put to them the gravy that is in the dish, a little butter and a spoonful of vinegar, so boil it up and put it in cups, and set them round the head upon the dish, take the tongue and blanch it, cut it in two, and lay it on each side the head, and some slices of crisp bacon over the head, so serve it up.

42. SAUCE *for a* NECK *of* VEAL.

Fry your veal, and when fried put in a little water, an anchovy, a few sweet herbs, a little onion, nutmeg, a little lemon-peel shred small, and a little white wine or ale, then shake it up with a little butter and flour, with some cockles and capers.

43. *To boil a* LEG *of* LAMB, *with the* LOYN *fry'd about it.*

When your lamb is boil'd lay it in the dish, and pour upon it a little parsley, butter and green gooseberries coddled, then lay your fried lamb round it; take some small asparagus and cut it small like peas, and boil it green; when it is boil'd drain it in a cullender, and lay it round your lamb in spoonfuls.

Garnish your dish with gooseberries, and heads of asparagus in lumps.

This is proper for a bottom dish.

44. *A* LEG *of* LAMB *boil'd with* CHICKENS *round it.*

When your lamb is boil'd pour over it parsley and butter, with coddled gooseberries, so lay the chickens round your lamb, and pour over the chickens a little white fricassy sauce. Garnish your dish with sippets and lemon.

This is proper for a top dish.

45. *A Fricassy of* LAMB *white.*

Take a leg of lamb, half roast it, when it is cold cut it in slices, put it into a stew-pan with a little white gravy, a shalot shred fine, a little nutmeg, salt, and a few shred capers; let it boil over the stove whilst the lamb is enough; to thicken your sauce, take three spoonfuls of cream, the yolks of two eggs, a little shred parsley, and beat them well together, then put it into your stew-pan and shake it whilst it is thick, but don't let it boil; if this do not make it thick, put in a little flour and butter, so serve it up. Garnish your dish with mushrooms, oysters and lemon.

46. *A brown Fricassy of* LAMB.

Take a leg of lamb, cut it in thin slices and season it with pepper and salt, then fry it brown with butter, when it is fried put it into your stew-pan, with a little brown gravy, an anchovy, a spoonful or two of white wine or claret, grate in a little nutmeg, and set it over the stove; thicken your sauce with flour and butter. Garnish your dish with mushrooms, oysters and lemon.

47. *To make* PIG *eat like* LAMB *in Winter.*

Take a pig about a month old and dress it, lay it down to the fire, when the skin begins to harden you must take it off by pieces, and when you have taken all the skin off, draw it and when it is cold cut it in quarters and lard it with parsley; then roast it for use.

48. *How to stew a* HARE.

Take a young hare, wash and wipe it well, cut the legs into two or three pieces, and all the other parts the same bigness, beat them all flat with a paste-pin, season it with nutmeg and salt, then flour it over, and fry it in butter over a quick fire; when you have fried it put into a stew-pan, with about a pint of gravy, two or three spoonfuls of claret and a small anchovy, so shake it up with butter and flour, (you must not let it boil in the stew-pan, for it will make it cut hard) then serve it up. Garnish your dish with crisp parsley.

49. *How to Jug a* HARE.

Take a young hare, cut her in pieces as you did for stewing, and beat it well, season it with the same seasoning you did before, put it into a pitcher or any other close pot, with half a pound of butter, set it in a pot of boiling water, stop up the pitcher close with a cloth, and lay upon it some weight for fear it should fall on one side; it will take about two hours in stewing; mind your pot be full of water, and keep it boiling all the time; when it is enough take the gravy from it, clear off the fat, and put her into your gravy in a stew-pan, with a spoonful or two of white wine, a little juice of lemon, shred lemon-peel and mace; you must thicken it up as you would a white fricassy.

Garnish your dish with sippets and lemon.

50. *To roast a* HARE *with a pudding in the belly.*

When you have wash'd the hare, nick the legs thro' the joints, and skewer them on both sides, which will keep her from drying in the roasting; when you have skewer'd her, put the pudding into her belly, baste her with nothing but butter: put a little in the dripping pan; you must not baste it with the water at all: when your hare is enough, take the gravy out of the dripping pan, and thicken it up with a little flour and butter for the sauce.

How to make a Pudding *for the* Hare.

Take the liver, a little beef-suet, sweet-marjoram and parsley shred small, with bread-crumbs and two eggs; season it with nutmeg, pepper and salt to your taste, mix all together and if it be too stiff put in a spoonful or two of cream: You must not boil the liver.

51. *To make a brown fricassy of* RABBETS.

Take a rabbet, cut the legs in three pieces, and the remainder of the rabbet the same bigness, beat them thin and fry them in butter over a quick fire; when they are fried put them into a stew-pan with a little gravy, a spoonful of catchup, and a little nutmeg; then shake it up with a little flour and butter.

Garnish your dish with crisp parsley.

52. *A white fricassy of* RABBETS.

Take a couple of young rabbets and half roast them; when they are cold take off the skin, and cut the rabbets in small pieces, (only take the white part) when you have cut it in pieces, put it into a stew-pan with white gravy, a small anchovy, a little onion, shred mace and lemon-peel, set it over a stove, and let it have one boil, then take a little cream, the yolks of two eggs, a lump of butter, a little juice of lemon and shred parsley; put them all together into a stew-pan, and shake them over the fire whilst they be as white as cream; you must not let it boil, if you do it will curdle. Garnish your dish with shred lemon and pickles.

53. *How to make pulled* RABBETS.

Take two young rabbets, boil them very tender, and take off all the white meat, and pull off the skin, then pull it all in shives, and put it into your stew-pan with a little white gravy, a spoonful of white wine, a little nutmeg and salt to your taste; thicken it up as you would a white fricassy, but put in no parsley; when you serve it up lay the heads in the middle. Garnish your dish with shred lemon and pickles.

54. *To dress Rabbets to look like* MOOR-GAME.

Take a young rabbet, when it is cased cut off the wings and the head; leave the neck of your rabbet as long as you can; when you case it you must leave on the feet, pull off the skin, leave on the claws, so double your rabbet and skewer it like a fowl; put a skewer at the bottom through the legs and neck, and tie it with a string, it will prevent its flying open; when you dish it up make the same sauce as you would do for partridges. Three are enough for one dish.

55. *To make white Scotch* COLLOPS.

Take about four pounds of a fillet of veal, cut it in small pieces as thin as you can, then take a stew-pan, butter it well over, and shake a little flour over it, then lay your meat in piece by piece, whilst all your pan be covered; take two or three blades of mace, and a little nutmeg, set your stew-pan over the fire, toss it up together 'till all your meat be white, then take half a pint of strong veal broth, which must be ready made, a quarter of a pint of cream, and the yolks of two eggs, mix all these together, put it to your meat, keeping it tossing all the time 'till they just boil up, then they are enough; the last thing you do squeeze in a little lemon: You may put in oysters, mushrooms, or what you will to make it rich.

56. *To boil* DUCKS *with* ONION SAUCE.

Take two fat ducks, and season them with a little pepper and salt, and skewer them up at both ends, and boil them whilst they are tender; take four or five large onions and boil them in milk and water, change the water two or three times in the boiling, when they are enough chop them very small, and rub them through a hair-sieve with the back of a spoon, 'till you have rubb'd them quite through, then melt a little butter, put in your onions and a little salt, and pour it upon your ducks. Garnish your dish with onions and sippets.

57. *To stew* DUCKS *either wild or tame.*

Take two ducks and half-roast them, cut them up as you would do for eating, then put them into a stew-pan with a little brown gravy, a glass of claret, two anchovies, a small onion shred very fine, and a little salt; thicken it up with flour and butter, so serve it up. Garnish you dish with a little raw onion and sippets.

58. *To make a white fricassy of* CHICKENS.

Take two or more chickens, half-roast them, cut them up as you would do for eating, and skin them; put them into a stew-pan with a little white gravy, juice of lemon, two anchovies, shred mace and nutmeg, then boil it; take the yolks of three eggs, a little sweet cream and shred parsley, put them into your stew-pan with a lump of butter and a little salt; shake them all the while they are over the stove, and be sure you do not let them boil lest they should curdle.

Garnish your dish with sippets and lemon.

59. *How to make a brown fricassy of* CHICKENS.

Take two or more chickens, as you would have your dish in bigness, cut them up as you do for eating, and flat them a little with a paste-pin; fry them a light-brown, and put them into your stew-pan with a little gravy, a spoonful or two of white wine, a little nutmeg and salt; thicken it up with flour and butter. Garnish your dish with sippets and crisp parsley.

60. CHICKENS SURPRISE.

Take half a pound of rice, set it over a fire in soft water, when it is half-boiled put in two or three small chickens truss'd, with two or three blades of mace, and a little salt; take a piece of bacon about three inches square, and boil it in water whilst almost enough, then take it out, pare off the outsides, and put it into the chickens and rice to boil a little together; (you must not let the broth be over thick with rice) then take up your chickens, lay them on a dish, pour over them the rice, cut your bacon in thin slices to lay round your chickens, and upon the breast of each a slice.

This is proper for a side-dish.

61. *To boil* CHICKENS.

Take four or five small chickens, as you would have your dish in bigness;

if they be small ones you may scald them, it will make them whiter; draw them, and take out the breast-bone before you scald them; when you have dress'd them, put them into milk and water, and wash them, truss them, and cut off the heads and necks; if you dress them the night before you use them, dip a cloth in milk and wrap them in it, which will make them white; you must boil them in milk and water, with a little salt; half an hour or less will boil them.

To make Sauce for the CHICKENS.

Take the necks, gizzards and livers, boil them in water, when they are enough strain off the gravy, and put to it a spoonful of oyster-pickle; take the livers, break them small, mix a little gravy, and rub them through a hair-sieve with the back of a spoon, then put to it a spoonful of cream, a little lemon and lemon-peel grated; thicken it up with butter and flour. Let your sauce be no thicker than cream, which pour upon your chickens. Garnish your dish with sippets, mushrooms, and slices of lemon.

They are proper for a side-dish or a top-dish either at noon or night.

62. *How to boil a* TURKEY.

When your turkey is dress'd and drawn, truss her, cut off her feet, take down the breast-bone with a knife, and sew up the skin again; stuff the breast with a white stuffing.

How to make the Stuffing. Take the sweet-bread of veal, boil it, shred it fine, with a little beef-suet, a handful of bread-crumbs, a little lemon-peel, part of the liver, a spoonful or two of cream, with nutmeg, pepper, salt, and two eggs, mix all together, and stuff your turkey with part of the stuffing, (the rest you may either boil or fry to lay round it) dridge it with a little flour, tie it up in a cloth, and boil it with milk and water: If it be a young turkey an hour will boil it.

How to make Sauce for the Turkey. Take a little small white gravy, a pint of oysters, two or three spoonfuls of cream, a little juice of lemon, and salt to your taste, thicken it up with flour and butter, then pour it over your turkey, and serve it up; lay round your turkey fry'd oysters, and the forc'd-meat. Garnish your dish with oysters, mushrooms, and slices of lemon.

63. *How to make another Sauce for a* Turkey.

Take a little strong white gravy, with some of the whitest sellery you can get, cut it about an inch long, boil it whilst it be tender, and put it into the gravy, with two anchovies, a little lemon-peel shred, two or three spoonfuls of cream, a little shred mace, and a spoonful of white wine; thicken it up with flour and butter; if you dislike the sellery you may put in the liver as you did for chickens.

64. *How to roast a* TURKEY.

Take a turkey, dress and truss it, then take down the breast-bone. *To make Stuffing for the Breast.* Take beef-suet, the liver shred fine, and bread-crumbs, a little lemon-peel, nutmeg, pepper and salt to your taste, a little shred parsley, a spoonful or two of cream, and two eggs. Put her on a spit and roast her before a slow fire; you may lard your turkey with fat bacon; if the turkey be young, an hour and a quarter will roast it. For the sauce, take a little white gravy, an onion, a few bread-crumbs, and a little whole pepper, let them boil well together, put to them a little flour and a lump of butter, which pour upon the turkey; you may lay round your turkey forc'd-meat-balls.

Garnish your dish with slices of lemon.

65. *To make a rich* TURKEY PIE.

Take a young turkey and bone her, only leave in the thigh bones and short pinions; take a large fowl and bone it, a little shred mace, nutmeg, pepper and salt, and season the turkey and fowl in the inside; lay the fowl in the inside of the low part of the turkey, and stuff the breast with a little white stuffing, (the same white stuffing as you made for the boiled turkey,) take a deep dish, lay a paste over it, and leave no paste in the bottom; lay in the turkey, and lay round it a few forc'd-meat-balls, put in half a pound of butter, and a jill of water, then close up the pie, an hour and a half will bake it; when it comes from the oven take off the lid, put in a pint of stew'd oysters, and the yolks of six or eight eggs, lay them at an equal distance round the turkey; you must not stew your oysters in gravy but in water, and pour them upon your turkey's breast; lay round six or eight artichoke-bottoms fry'd, so serve it up without the lid; you must take the fat out of the pie before you put in the oysters.

66. *To make a* TURKEY *A-la-Daube.*

Take a large turkey and truss it; take down the breast-bone, and stuff it in the breast with some stuffing, as you did the roast turkey, lard it with bacon, then rub the skin of the turkey with the yolk of an egg, and strow over it a little nutmeg, pepper, salt, and a few bread-crumbs, then put it into a copper-dish and fend it to the oven; when you dish it up make for the turkey brown gravy-sauce; shred into your sauce a few oysters and mushrooms; lay round artichoke-bottoms fry'd, stew'd pallets, forc'd-meat-balls, and a little crisp bacon. Garnish your dish with pickled mushrooms, and slices of lemon.

This is a proper dish for a remove.

67. POTTED TURKEY.

Take a turkey, bone her as you did for the pie, and season it very well in the inside and outside with mace, nutmeg, pepper and salt, then put it into a pot that you design to keep it in, put over it a pound of butter, when it is baked draw from it the gravy, and take off the fat, then squeeze it down very tight in the pot; and to keep it down lay upon it a weight; when it's cold take part of the butter that came from it, and clarify a little more with it to cover your turkey, and keep it in a cool place for use; you may put a fowl in the belly if you please.

Ducks or geese are potted the same way.

68. *How to jugg* PIGEONS.

Take six or eight pigeons and truss them, season them with nutmeg, pepper and salt. *To make the Stuffing.* Take the livers and shred them with beef-suet, bread-crumbs, parsley, sweet-marjoram, and two eggs, mix all together, then stuff your pigeons sowing them up at both ends, and put them into your jugg with the breast downwards, with half a pound of butter; stop up the jugg close with a cloth that no steam can get out, then set them in a pot of water to boil; they will take above two hours stewing; mind you keep your pot full of water, and boiling all the time; when they are enough clear from them the gravy, and take the fat clean off; put to your gravy a spoonful of cream, a little lemon-peel, an anchovy shred, a few mushrooms, and a little white wine, thicken it with a little flour and butter, then dish up your pigeons, and pour over them the sauce. Garnish the dish with mushrooms and slices of lemon.

This is proper for a side dish.

69. MIRRANADED PIGEONS.

Take six pigeons, and truss them as you would do for baking, break the breast-bones, season and stuff them as you did for jugging, put them into a little deep dish and lay over them half a pound of butter; put into your dish a little water. Take half a pound of rice, cree it soft as you would do for eating, and pour it upon the back of a sieve, let it stand while it is cold, then take a spoon and flat it like paste on your hand, and lay on the breast of every pigeon a cake; lay round your dish some puff-paste not over thin, and send them to the oven; about half an hour will bake them.

This is proper at noon for a side-dish.

70. *To stew* PIGEONS.

Take your pigeons, season and stuff them, flat the breast-bone, and truss them up as you would do for baking, dredge them over with a little flour, and fry them in butter, turning them round till all sides be brown, then put them into a stew-pan with as much brown gravy as will cover them, and let them stew whilst your pigeons be enough; then take part of the gravy, an anchovy shred, a little catchup, a small onion, or a shalot, and a little juice of lemon for sauce, pour it over your pigeons, and lay round them forc'd-meat-balls and crisp bacon. Garnish your dish with crisp parsley and lemon.

71. *To broil* PIGEONS *whole*.

Take your pigeons, season and stuff them with the same stuffing you did jugg'd pigeons, broil them either before a fire or in an oven; when they are enough take the gravy from them, and take off the fat, then put to the gravy two or three spoonfuls of water, a little boil'd parsley shred, and thicken your sauce. Garnish your dish with crisp parsley.

72. *Boiled* PIGEONS *with fricassy Sauce*.

Take your pigeons, and when you have drawn and truss'd them up, break the breast bone, and lay them in milk and water to make them white, tie them in a cloth and boil them in milk and water; when you dish them up put to them white fricassy sauce, only adding a few shred mushrooms. Garnish with crisp parsley and sippets.

73. *To Pot* PIGEONS.

Take your pigeons and skewer them with their feet cross over the breast, to stand up; season them with pepper and salt, and roast them; so put them into your pot, setting the feet up; when they are cold cover them up with clarified butter.

74. *To stew* PALLETS.

Take three or four large beast pallets and boil them very tender, blanch and cut them in long pieces the length of your finger, then in small bits the cross way; shake them up with a little good gravy and a lump of butter; season them with a little nutmeg and salt, put in a spoonful of white wine, and thicken it with the yolks of eggs as you do, a white fricassy.

75. *To make a Fricassy of* PIG'S EARS.

Take three or four pig's ears as large as you would have your dish in bigness, clean and boil them very tender, cut them in small pieces the length of your finger, and fry them with butter till they be brown; so put them into a stew-pan with a little brown gravy, a lump of butter, a spoonful of vinegar, and a little mustard and salt, thicken'd with flour; take two or three pig's feet and boil them very tender, fit for eating, then cut them in two and take out the large bones, dip them in egg, and strew over them a few bread-crumbs, season them with pepper and salt; you may either fry or broil them, and lay them in the middle of your dish with the pig's ears.

They are proper for a side-dish.

76. *To make a Fricassy of* TRIPES.

Take the whitest seam tripes you can get and cut them in long pieces, put them into a stew-pan with a little good gravy, a few bread-crumbs, a lump of butter, a little vinegar to your taste, and a little mustard if you like it; shake it up altogether with a little shred parsley. Garnish your dish with sippets.

This is proper for a side-dish.

77. *To make a Fricassy of* VEAL-SWEET-BREADS.

Take five or six veal-sweet-breads, according as you would have your dish in bigness, and boil them in water, cut them in thin slices the length-way, dip them in egg, season them with pepper and salt, fry them a light brown; then put them into a stew-pan with a little brown gravy, a spoonful of white wine or juice of lemon, whether you please; thicken it up with flour and butter; and serve it up. Garnish your dish with crisp parsley.

78. *To make a white Fricassy of* TRIPES, *to eat like* CHICKENS.

Take the whitest and the thickest seam tripe you can get, cut the white part in thin slices, put it into a stew-pan with a little white gravy, juice of lemon and lemon-peel shred, also a spoonful of white wine; take the yolks of two or three eggs and beat them very well, put to them a little thick cream, shred parsley, and two or three chives if you have any; shake altogether over the stove while it be as thick as cream, but don't let it boil for fear it curdle. Garnish your dish with sippets, slic'd lemon or mushrooms, and serve it up.

79. *To make a brown Fricassy of* EGGS.

Take eight or ten eggs, according to the bigness you design your dish, boil them hard, put them in water, take off the shell, fry them in butter whilst they be a deep brown, put them into a stew-pan with a little brown gravy, and a lump of butter, so thicken it up with flour; take two or three eggs, lay them in the middle of the dish, then take the other, cut them in two, and set them with the small ends upwards round the dish; fry some sippets and lay round them. Garnish your dish with crisp parsley.

This is proper for a side-dish in lent

80. *To make a white Fricasy of* EGGS.

Take ten or twelve eggs, boil them hard and pill them, put them in a stew-pan with a little white gravy; take the yolks of two or three eggs, beat them very well, and put to them two or three spoonfuls of cream, a spoonful of white wine, a little juice of lemon, shred parsley, and salt to your taste; shake altogether over the stove till it be as thick as cream, but don't let it boil; take your eggs and lay one part whole on the dish, the rest cut in halves and quarters, and lay them round your dish; you must not cut them till you lay them on the dish. Garnish your dish with sippets, and serve it up.

81. *To stew* EGGS *in* GRAVY.

Take a little gravy, pour it into a little pewter dish, and set it over a stove, when it is hot break in as many eggs as will cover the dish bottom, keep pouring the gravy over them with a spoon 'till they are white at the top, when they are enough strow over them a little salt; fry some square sippets of bread in butter, prick them with the small ends upward, and serve them up.

82. *How to Collar a* PIECE *of* BEEF *to eat Cold.*

Take a flank of beef or pale-board, which you can get, bone them and take off the inner skin; nick your beef about an inch distance, but mind you don't cut thro' the skin of the outside; then take two ounces of saltpetre, and beat it small, and take a large handful of common salt and mix them together, first sprinkling your beef over with a little water, and lay it in an earthen dish, then strinkle over your salt, so let it stand, four or five days, then take a pretty large quantity of all sorts of mild sweet herbs, pick and shred them very small, take some bacon and cut it in long pieces the thickness of your finger, then take your beef and lay one layer of bacon in every nick; and another of the greens; when you have done season your beef with a little beat mace, pepper, salt and nutmeg; you may add a little neat's tongue, and an anchovy in some of the nicks; so roll it up tight, bind it in a cloth with coarse inkle round it, put it into a large stew-pot and cover it with water; let the beef lie with the end downwards, put to the pickle that was in the beef when it lay in salt, set it in a slow oven all the night, then take it out and bind it tight, and tie up both ends, the next day take it out of the cloth, and put it into pickle; you must take off the fat and boil the pickle, put in a handful of salt, a few bay leaves, a little whole Jamaica and black pepper, a quart of stale strong beer, a little vinegar and alegar; if you make the pickle very good, it will keep five or six months very well; if your beef be not too much baked it will cut all in diamonds.

83. *To roll a* BREAST OF VEAL *to eat cold.*

Take a large breast of veal, fat and white, bone it and cut it in two, season it with mace, nutmeg, pepper and salt, in one part you may strinkle a few sweet herbs shred fine, roll them tight up, bind them will with coarse ickle, so boil it an hour and a half; you may make the same pickle as you did for the beef, excepting the strong beer; when it is enough to take it up, and bind it as you did the beef, so hang it up whilst it be cold.

84. *To pot* TONGUES.

Take your tongues and salt them with saltpetre, common salt and bay salt, let them lie ten days, then take them out and boil them whilst they will blanch, cut off the lower part of the tongues, then season them with mace, pepper, nutmeg and salt, put them into a pot and send them to the oven, and the low part of your tongues that you cut off lay upon your tongues, and one pound of butter, then let them bake whilst they are tender, then take them out of the pot, throw over them a little more seasoning, put them into the pot you design to keep them in, press them down very tight, lay over them a weight, and let them stand all night, then cover them with clarified butter: You must not salt your tongues as you do for hanging.

85. *How to pot* VENISON.

Take your venison and cut it in thin pieces, season it with pepper and salt, put it into your pot, lay over it some butter and a little beef-suet, let it stand all night in the oven; when it is baked beat them in a marble mortar or wooden-bowl, put in part of the gravy, and all the fat you take from it; when you have beat it put into your pot, then take the fat lap of a shoulder of mutton, take off the out-skin, and roast it, when it is roasted and cold, cut it in long pieces the thickness of your finger; when you put the venison into the pot, put it in at three times, betwixt every one lay the mutton cross your pot, at an equal distance; if you cut it the right way it will cut all in diamonds; leave some of the venison to lay on the top, and cover it with clarified butter; to keep it for use.

86. *To pot all Sorts of* WILD-FOWL.

When the wild-fowl are dressed take a paste-pin, and beat them on the breast 'till they are flat; before you roast them season them with mace, nutmeg, pepper and salt; you must not roast them over much; when you draw them season them on the out-side, and set them on one end to drain out the gravy, and put them into your pot; you may put in two layers; if you press them very flat, cover them with clarified butter when they are cold.

87. *How to pot* BEEF.

Take two pounds of the slice or buttock, season it with about two ounces of saltpetre and a little common salt, let it lie two or three days, send it to the oven, and season it with a little pepper, salt and mace; lay over your beef half a pound of butter or beef suet, and let it stand all night in the oven to stew; take from it the gravy and the butter, and beat them (with the beef) in a bowl, then take a quarter of a pound of anchovies, bone them, and beat them too with a little of the gravy; if it be not seasoned enough to your taste, put to it a little more seasoning; put is close down in a pot, and when it is cold cover it up with butter, and keep it for use.

88. *To Ragoo a* RUMP *of* BEEF.

Take a rump of beef, lard it with bacon and spices, betwixt the larding, stuff it with forced meat, made of a pound of veal, three quarters of a pound of beef-suet, a quarter of a pound of fat bacon boiled and shred well by itself, a good quantity of parsley, winter savoury, thyme, sweet-marjoram, and an onion, mix all this together, season it with mace cloves, cinnamon, salt, Jamaica and black pepper, and some grated bread, work the forc'd-meat up with three whites and two yolks of eggs, then stuff it, and lay some rough suet in a stew pan with your beef upon it, let it fry till it be brown then put in some water, a bunch of sweet herbs, a large onion stuffed with cloves, sliced turnips, carrots cut as large as the yolk of an egg, some whole pepper and salt, half a pint of claret, cover it close, and let it stew six or seven hours over a gentle fire, turning it very often.

89. *How to make a* SAUCE *for it.*

Take truffles, morels, sweet-breads, diced pallets boiled tender, three anchovies, and some lemon-peel, put these into some brown gravy and stew them; if you do not think it thick enough, dredge in a little flour, and just before you pour it on your beef put in a little white wine and vinegar, and serve it up hot.

90. *Sauce for boiled* RABBETS.

Take a few onions, boil them thoroughly, shifting them in water often, mix them well together with a little melted butter and water. Some add a little pulp of apple and mustard.

91. *To salt a* Leg *of* Mutton *to eat like* Ham.

Take a leg of mutton, an ounce of saltpetre, two ounces of bay-salt, rub it in very well, take a quarter of a pound of coarse sugar, mix it with two or three handfuls of common salt, then take and salt it very well, and let it lie a week, so hang it up, and keep it for use, after it is dry use it, the sooner the better; it won't keep so long as ham.

92. *How to salt* HAM *or* TONGUES.

Take a middling ham, two ounces of saltpetre, a quarter of a pound of bay-salt, beat them together, and rub them on your ham very well, before you salt it on the inside, set your salt before the fire to warm; to every ham take half a pound of coarse sugar, mix to it a little of the salt, and rub it in very well, let it lie for a week or ten days, then salt it again very well, and let it lie another week or ten days, then hang it to dry, not very near the fire, nor over much in the air.

Take your tongues and clean them, and cut off the root, then take two ounces of saltpetre, a quarter of a pound of bay-salt well beaten, three or four tongues, according as they are in bigness, lay them on a thing by themselves, for if you lay them under your bacon it flats your tongues, and spoils them; salt them very well, and let them lie as long as the hams with the skin side downwards: You may do a rump of beef the same way, only leave out the sugar.

[Note: The text for the next three recipes—93, 94 and 95—was missing from our scans. Only the last part of recipe number 95 is available.]

93.

94.

95. … bacon, you may put in two or three slices when you send them to the oven.

96. *How to make a* HARE-PIE.

Parboil the hare, take out the bones, and beat the meat in a mortar with some fat pork or new bacon, then soak it in claret all night, the next day take it out, season it with pepper, salt and nutmeg, then lay the back bone into the middle of the pie, put the meat about it with about three quarters of a pound of butter, and bake it in a puff-paste, but lay no paste in the bottom of the dish.

97. *To make a* HARE-PIE *another Way.*

Take the flesh of a hare after it is skined, and string it: take a pound of beef-suet or marrow shred small, with sweet-marjoram, parsley and shalots, take the hare, cut it in pieces, season it with mace, pepper, salt and nutmeg, then bake it either in cold or hot paste, and when it is baked, open it and put to it some melted butter.

98. *To make* PIG *Royal.*

Take a pig and roast it the same way as you did for lamb, when you draw it you must not cut it up, when it is cold you must lard it with bacon, cut not your layers too small, if you do they will melt away, cut them about an inch and a quarter long; you must put one row down the back, and one on either side, then strinkle it over with a few bread-crumbs and a little salt, and set it in the oven, an hour will bake it, but mind your oven be not too hot; you must take another pig of a less size, roast it, cut it up, and lie it on each side: The sauce you make for a roast pig will serve for both.

This is proper for a bottom dish at a grand entertainment.

99. *To roast* VEAL *a savoury Way.*

When you have stuffed your veal, strow some of the ingredients over it; when it is roasted make your sauce of what drops from the meat, put an anchovy in water, and when dissolved pour it into the dripping-pan with a large lump of butter and oysters: toss it up with flour to thicken it.

100. *To make a* HAM PIE.

Cut the ham round, and lay it in water all night, boil it tender as you would do for eating, take off the skin, strew over it a little pepper, and bake it in a deep dish, put to it a pint of water, and half a pound of butter; you must bake it in puff-paste; but lay no paste in the bottom of the dish; when you send it to the table send it without a lid.

It is proper for a top or bottom dish either summer or winter.

101. *To make a* NEAT's TONGUE PIE.

Take two or three tongues, (according as you would have your pie in bigness) cut off the roots and low parts, take two ounces of saltpetre, a little bay salt, rub them very well, lay them on an earthen dish with the skin side downwards, let them lie for a week or ten days, whilst they be very red, then boil them as tender as you would have them for eating blanch and season with a little pepper and salt, flat them as much as you can, bake them in puff paste in a deep dish, but lay no paste in the bottom, put to them a little gravy, and half a pound of butter; lay your tongues with the wrong side upwards, when they are baked turn them, and serve it up without a lid.

102. *To broil* SHEEP *or* HOG's TONGUES.

Boil, blanch, and split your tongues, season them with a little pepper and salt, then dip them in egg, strow over them a few bread-crumbs, and broil them whilst they be brown; serve them up with a little gravy and butter.

103. *To Pickle* PORK.

Cut off the leg, shoulder pieces, the bloody neck and the spare-rib as bare as you can, then cut the middle pieces as large as they can lie in the tub, salt them with saltpetre, bay-salt, and white salt; your saltpetre must be beat small, and mix'd with the other salts; half a peck of white salt, a quart of bay-salt, and half a pound of saltpetre, is enough for a large hog; you must rub the pork very well with your salt, then lay a thick layer of salt all over the tub, then a piece of pork, and do so till all your pork is in; lay the skin side downwards, fill up all the hollows and sides of the tub with little pieces that are not bloody press all down as close as possible, and lay on a good layer of salt on the top, then lay on the legs and shoulder pieces, which must be used first, the rest will keep two years if not pulled up, nor the pickle poured from it. You must observe to see it covered with pickle.

104. *To fricassy* CALF'S FEET *white.*

Dress the calf's feet, boil them as you would do for eating, take out the long bones, cut them in two, and put them into a stew-pan with a little white gravy, and a spoonful or two of white wine; take the yolks of two or three eggs, two or three spoonfuls of cream, grate in a little nutmeg and salt, and shake all together with a lump of butter. Garnish your dish with slices of lemon and currans, and so serve them up.

105. *To roll a* PIG'S *Head to eat like Brawn.*

Take a large pig's head, cut off the groin ends, crack the bones and put it in water, shift it once or twice, cut off the ears, then boil it so tender that the bones will slip out, nick it with a knife in the thick part of the head, throw over it a pretty large handful of salt; take half a dozen of large neat's feet, boil them while they be soft, split them, and take out all the bones and black bits; take a strong coarse cloth, and lay the feet with the skin side downwards, with all the loose pieces in the inside; press them with your hand to make them of an equal thickness, lay them at that length that they will reach round the head, and throw over them a handful of salt, then lay the head across, one thick part one way and the other another, that the fat may appear alike at both ends; leave one foot out to lay at the top to make a lantern to reach round, bind it with filleting as you would do brawn, and tie it very close at both ends; you may take it out of the cloth the next day, take off the filleting and wash it, wrap it about again very tight, and keep it in brawn-pickle.

This has been often taken for real Brawn.

106. *How to fry* CALF'S FEET *in Butter.*

Take four Calf's feet and blanch them, boil them as you would do for eating, take out the large bones and cut them in two, beat a spoonful of wheat flour and four eggs together, put to it a little nutmeg, pepper and salt, dip in your calf's feet, and fry them in butter a light brown, and lay them upon your dish with a little melted butter over them. Garnish with slices of lemon and serve them up.

107. *How to make* SAVOURY PATTEES.

Take the kidney of a loyn of veal before it be roasted, cut it in thin slices, season it with mace, pepper and salt, and make your pattees; lay in every patty a slice, and either bake or fry them.

You may make marrow pattees the same way.

108. *To make* EGG PIES.

Take and boil half a dozen eggs, half a dozen apples, a pound and a half of beef-suet, a pound of currans, and shred them, so season it with mace, nutmeg and sugar to your taste, a spoonful or two of brandy, and sweet meats, if you please.

109. *To make a sweet* CHICKEN PIE.

Break the chicken bones, cut them in little bits, season them lightly with mace and salt, take the yolks of four eggs boiled hard and quartered, five artichoke-bottoms, half a pound of sun raisins stoned, half a pound of citron, half a pound of lemon, half a pound of marrow, a few forc'd-meat-balls, and half a pound of currans well cleaned, so make a light puff-paste, but put no paste in the bottom; when it is baked take a little white wine, a little juice of either orange or lemon, the yolk of an egg well beat, and mix them together, make it hot and put it into your pie; when you serve it up take the same ingredients you use for a lamb or veal pie, only leave out the artichokes.

110. *To roast* TONGUES.

Cut off the roots of two tongues, take three ounces of saltpetre, a little bay-salt and common salt, rub them very well, let them lie a week or ten days to make them red, but not salt, so boil them tender as they will blanch, strow over them a few bread crumbs, set them before the fire to brown on every side.

To make SAUCE *for the* TONGUES.

Take a few bread crumbs, and as much water as will wet them, then put in claret till they be red, and a little beat cinnamon, sweeten it to your taste, put a little gravy on the dish with your tongues, and the sweet sauce in two basons, set them on each side, so serve them up.

111. *To fry* CALF'S FEET *in Eggs.*

Boil your calf's feet as you would do for eating, take out the long bones and split them in two, when they are cold season 'em with a little pepper, salt and nutmeg; take three eggs, put to them a spoonful of flour, so dip the feet in it and fry them in butter; you must have a little gravy and butter for sauce. Garnish with currans, so serve them up.

112. *To make a* MINC'D PIE *of Calf's Feet.*

Take two or three calf's feet, and boil them as you would do for eating, take out the long bones, shred them very fine, put to them double their weight of beef-suet shred fine, and about a pound of currans well cleaned, a quarter of a pound of candid orange and citron cut in small pieces, half a pound of sugar, a little salt, a quarter of an ounce of mace and a large nutmeg, beat them together, put in a little juice of lemon or verjuice to your taste, a glass of mountain wine or sack, which you please, so mix all together; bake them in puff-paste.

113. *To roast a* WOODCOCK.

When you have dress'd your woodcock, and drawn it under the leg, take out the bitter bit, put in the trales again; whilst the woodcock is roasting set under it an earthen dish with either water in or small gravy, let the woodcock drop into it, take the gravy and put to it a little butter, and thicken it with flour; your woodcock will take about ten minutes roasting if you have a brisk fire; when you dish it up lay round it wheat bread toasts, and pour the sauce over the toasts, and serve it up.

You may roast a partridge the same way, only add crumb sauce in a bason.

114. *To make a* CALF'S HEAD PIE.

Take a calf's head and clean it, boil it as you would do for hashing, when it is cold cut it in thin slices, and season it with a little black pepper, nutmeg, salt, a few shred capers, a few oysters and cockles, two or three mushrooms, and green lemon-peel, mix them all well together, put them into your pie; it must be a standing pie baked in a flat pewter dish, with a rim of puff-paste round the edge; when you have filled the pie with the meat, lay on forc'd-meat-balls, and the yolks of some hard eggs, put in a little small gravy and butter; when it comes from the oven take off the lid, put into it a little white wine to your taste, and shake up the pie, so serve it up without lid.

115. *To make a* CALF'S FOOT PIE.

Take two or three calf's feet, according as you would have your pie in bigness, boil and bone them as you would do for eating, and when cold cut them in thin slices; take about three quarters of a pound of beef-suet shred fine, half a pound of raisins stoned, half a pound of cleaned currans, a little mace and nutmeg, green lemon-peel, salt, sugar, and candid lemon or orange, mix altogether, and put them in a dish, make a good puff-paste, but let there be no paste in the bottom of the dish; when it is baked, take off the lid, and squeeze in a little lemon or verjuice, cut the lid in sippets and lay round.

116. *To make a* WOODCOCK PIE.

Take three or four brace of woodcocks, according as you would have the pie in bigness, dress and skewer them as you would do for roasting, draw them, and season the inside with a little pepper, salt and mace, but don't wash them, put the trales into the belly again, but nothing else, for there is something in them that gives them a more bitterish taste in the baking than in the roasting, when you put them into the dish lay them with the breast downwards, beat them upon the breast as flat as you can; you must season them on the outside as you do the inside; bake them in puff-paste, but lay none in the bottom of the dish, put to them a jill of gravy and a little butter; you must be very careful your pie be not too much baked; when you serve it up take off the lid and turn the woodcocks with the breast upwards.

You may bake partridge the same way.

117. *To pickle* PIGEONS.

Take your pigeons and bone them; you must begin to bone them at the neck and turn the skin downwards, when they are boned season them with pepper, salt and nutmeg, sew up both ends, and boil them in water and white wine vinegar, a few bay leaves, a little whole pepper and salt; when they are enough take them out of the pickle, and boil it down with a little more salt, when it is cold put in the pigeons and keep them for use.

118. *To make a sweet* VEAL PIE.

Take a loin of veal, cut off the thin part length ways, cut the rest in thin slices, as much as you have occasion for, flat it with your bill, and cut off the bone ends next the chine, season it with nutmeg and salt; take half a pound of raisins stoned, and half a pound of currans well clean'd, mix all together, and lay a few of them at the bottom of the dish, lay a layer of meat; and betwixt every layer lay on your fruit, but leave some for the top; you must make a puff-paste; but lay none in the bottom of the dish; when you have filled your pie, put in a jill of water and a little butter, when it is baked have a caudle to put into it.

To make the caudle, see in receipt 177.

119. MINC'D PIES *another way*.

Take a pound of the finest seam tripes you can get, a pound and a half of currans well cleaned, two, three or four apples pared and shred very fine, a little green lemon-peel and mace shred, a large nutmeg, a glass of sack or brandy, (which you please) half a pound of sugar, and a little salt, so mix them well together, and fill your patty-pans, then stick five or six bits of candid lemon or orange in every petty-pan, cover them, and when baked they are fit for use.

120. *To make a savoury* CHICKEN PIE.

Take half a dozen small chickens, season them with mace, pepper and salt, both inside and out; then take three or four veal sweet-breads, season them with the same, and lay round them a few forc'd-meat-balls, put in a little water and butter; take a little white sweet gravy not over strong, shred a few oysters if you have any, and a little lemon-peel, squeeze in a little lemon juice, not to make it sour; if you have no oysters take the whitest of your sweet breads and boil them, cut them small, and put them in your gravy, thicken it with a little butter and flour; when you open the pie, if there is any fat, skim it off, and pour the sauce over the chicken breasts; so serve it up without lid.

121. *To roast a* HANCH *of* VENISON.

Take a hanch of venison and spit it, then take a little bread meal, knead and roll it very thin, lay it over the fat part of your venison with a paper over it, tye it round your venison, with a pack-thread; if it be a large hanch it will take four hours roasting, and a midling hanch three hours; keep it basting all the time you roast it; when you dish it up put a little gravy in the dish and sweet sauce in a bason; half an hour before you draw your venison take off the paste, baste it, and let it be a light brown.

122. *To make sweet* PATTEES.

Take the kidney of a loin of veal with the fat, when roasted shred it very fine, put to it a little shred mace, nutmeg and salt, about half a pound of currans, the juice of a lemon, and sugar to your taste, then bake them in puff-paste; you may either fry or bake them.

They are proper for a side-dish.

123. *To make* BEEF-ROLLS.

Cut your beef thin as for scotch collops, beat it very well, and season it with salt, Jamaica and white pepper, mace, nutmeg, sweet marjoram, parsley, thyme, and a little onion shred small, rub them on the collops on one side, then take long bits of beef-suet and roll in them, tying them up with a thread; flour them well, and fry them in butter very brown; then have ready some good gravy and stew them an hour and half, stirring them often, and keep them covered, when they are enough take off the threads, and put in a little flour, with a good lump of butter, and squeeze in some lemon, then they are ready for use.

124. *To make a* HERRING-PIE *of* WHITE SALT HERRINGS.

Take five or six salt herrings, wash them very well, lay them in a pretty quantity of water all night to take out the saltness, season them with a little black pepper, three or four middling onions pill'd and shred very fine lay one part of them at the bottom of the pie, and the other at the top; to five or six herrings put in half a pound of butter, then lay in your herrings whole, only take off the heads; make them into a standing pie with a thin crust.

125. *How to* COLLAR PIG.

Take a large pig that is fat, about a month old, kill and dress it, cut off the head, cut it in two down the back and bone it, then cut it in three or four pieces, wash it in a little water to take out the blood: take a little milk and water just warm, put in your pig, let it lie about a day and a night, shift it two or three times in that time to make it white, then take it out and wipe it very well with a dry cloth, and season it with mace, nutmeg, pepper and salt; take a little shred of parsley and strinkle over two of the quarters, so roll them up in a fine soft cloth, tie it up at both ends, bind it tight with a little filletting or coarse inkle, and boil it in milk and water with a little salt; it will take about an hour and a half boiling; when it is enough bind it up tight in your cloth again, hang it up whilst it be cold. For the pickle boil a little milk and water, a few bay leaves and a little salt; when it is cold take your pig out of the cloths and put it into the pickle; you must shift it out of your pickle two or three times to make it white, the last pickle make strong, and put in a little whole pepper, a pretty large handful of salt, a few bay leaves, and so keep it for use.

126. *To* COLLAR SALMON.

Take the side of a middling salmon, and cut off the head, take out all the bones and the outside, season it with mace, nutmeg, pepper and salt, roll it tight up in a cloth, boil it, and bind it up with pickle; it will take about an hour boiling; when it is boiled bind it tight again, when cold take it very carefully out of the cloth and bind it about with filleting; you must not take off the filleting but as it is eaten.

To make PICKLE *to keep it in*.

Take two or three quarts of water, a jill of vinegar, a little Jamaica pepper and whole pepper, a large handful of salt, boil them altogether, and when it is cold put in your salmon, so keep it for use: If your pickle don't keep you must renew it.

You may collar pike the same way.

127. *To make an* OYSTER PIE.

Take a pint of the largest oysters you can get, clean them very well in their own liquor, if you have not liquor enough, add to them three or four spoonfuls of water; take the kidney of a loin of veal, cut it in thin slices, and season it with a little pepper and salt, lay the slices in the bottom of the dish, (but there must be no paste in the bottom of the dish) cover them with the oysters, strow over a little of the seasoning as you did for the veal; take the marrow of one or two bones, lay it over your oysters and cover them with puff-paste; when it is baked take off the lid, put into it a spoonful or two of white wine, shake it up altogether, and serve it up.

It is proper for a side dish, either for noon or night.

128. *To butter* CRAB *and* LOBSTER.

Dress all the meat out of the belly and claws of your lobster, put it into a stew-pan, with two or three spoonfuls of water, a spoonful or two of white wine vinegar, a little pepper, shred mace, and a lump of butter, shake it over the stove till it be very hot, but do not let it boil, if you do it will oil; put it into your dish, and lay round it your small claws:—it is as proper to put it in scallop shells as on a dish.

129. *To roast a* LOBSTER.

If your lobster be alive tie it to the spit, roast and baste it for half an hour; if it be boiled you must put it in boiling water, and let it have one boil, then lie it in a dripping-pan and baste it; when you lay it upon the dish split the tail, and lay it on each side, so serve it up with melted butter in a china cup.

130. *To make a* QUAKING PUDDING.

Take eight eggs and beat them very well, put to them three spoonfuls of London flour, a little salt, three jills of cream, and boil it with a stick of cinnamon and a blade of mace; when it is cold mix it to your eggs and flour, butter your cloth, and do not give it over much room in your cloth; about half an hour will boil it; you must turn it in the boiling or the flour will settle, so serve it up with a little melted butter.

131. *A* HUNTING PUDDING.

Take a pound of fine flour, a pound of beef-suet shred fine, three quarters of a pound of currans well cleaned, a quartern of raisins stoned and shred, five eggs, a little lemon-peel shred fine, half a nutmeg grated, a jill of cream, a little salt, about two spoonfuls of sugar, and a little brandy, so mix all well together, and tie it up right in your cloth; it will take two hours boiling; you must have a little white wine and butter for your sauce.

132. *A* CALF'S-FOOT PUDDING.

Take two calf's feet, when they are clean'd boil them as you would for eating; take out all the bones; when they are cold shred them in a wooden bowl as small as bread crumbs; then take the crumbs of a penny loaf, three quarters of a pound of beef suet shred fine, grate in half a nutmeg, take half a pound of currans well washed, half a pound of raisins stoned and shred, half a pound of sugar, six eggs, and a little salt, mix them all together very well, with as much cream as will wet them, so butter your cloth and tie it up tight; it will take two hours boiling; you may if you please stick it with a little orange, and serve it up.

133. *A* SAGOO PUDDING.

Take three or four ounces of sagoo, and wash it in two or three waters, set it on to boil in a pint of water, when you think it is enough take it up, set it to cool, and take half of a candid lemon shred fine, grate in half of a nutmeg, mix two ounces of jordan almonds blanched, grate in three ounces of bisket if you have it, if not a few bread-crumbs grated, a little rose-water and half a pint of cream; then take six eggs, leave out two of the whites, beat them with a spoonful or two of sack, put them to your sagoo, with about half a pound of clarified butter, mix them all together, and sweeten it with fine sugar, put in a little salt, and bake it in a dish with a little puff-paste about the dish edge, when you serve it up you may stick a little citron or candid orange, or any sweetmeats you please.

134. *A* MARROW PUDDING.

Take a penny loaf, take off the outside, then cut one half in thin slices; take the marrow of two bones, half a pound of currans well cleaned, shred your marrow, and strinkle a little marrow and currans over the dish; if you have not marrow enough you may add to it a little beef-suet shred fine; take five eggs and beat them very well, put to them three jills of milk, grate in half a nutmeg, sweeten it to your taste, mix all together, pour it over your pudding, and save a little marrow to strinkle over the top of your pudding; when you send it to the oven lye a puff-paste around the dish edge.

135. *A* CARROT PUDDING.

Take three or four clear red carrots, boil and peel them, take the red part of the carrot, beat it very fine in a marble mortar, put to it the crumbs of a penny loaf, six eggs, half a pound of clarified butter, two or three spoonfuls of rose water, a little lemon-peel shred, grate in a little nutmeg, mix them well together, bake it with a puff-paste round your dish, and have a little white wine, butter and sugar, for the sauce.

136. *A* GROUND RICE PUDDING.

Take half a pound of ground rice, half cree it in a quart of milk, when it is cold put to it five eggs well beat, a jill of cream, a little lemon-peel shred fine, half a nutmeg grated, half a pound of butter, and half a pound of sugar, mix them well together, put them into your dish with a little salt, and bake it with a puff-paste round your dish; have a little rose-water, butter and sugar to pour over it, you may prick in it candid lemon or citron if you please.

Half of the above quantity will make a pudding for a side-dish.

137. *A* POTATOE PUDDING.

Take three or four large potatoes, boil them as you would do for eating, beat them with a little rose-water and a glass of sack in a marble mortar, put to them half a pound of sugar, six eggs, half a pound of melted butter, half a pound of currans well cleaned, a little shred lemon-peel, and candid orange, mix altogether and serve it up.

138. *An* APPLE PUDDING.

Take half a dozen large codlins, or pippens, roast them and take out the pulp; take eight eggs, (leave out six of the whites) half a pound of fine powder sugar, beat your eggs and sugar well together, and put to them the pulp of your apples, half a pound of clarified butter, a little lemon-peel shred fine, a handful of bread crumbs or bisket, four ounces of candid orange or citron, and bake it with a thin paste under it.

139. *An* ORANGE PUDDING.

Take three large seville oranges, the clearest kind you can get, grate off the out-rhine; take eight eggs, (leave out six of the whites) half a pound of double refin'd sugar, beat and put it to your eggs, then beat them both together for half an hour; take three ounces of sweet almonds blanch'd, beat them with a spoonful or two of fair water to keep them from oiling, half a pound of butter, melt it without water, and the juice of two oranges, then put in the rasping of your oranges, and mix all together; lay a thin paste over your dish and bake it, but not in too hot an oven.

140. *An* ORANGE PUDDING *another Way.*

Take half a pound of candid orange, cut them in thin slices, and beat them in a marble mortar to a pulp; take six eggs, (leave out half of the whites) half a pound of butter, and the juice of one orange; mix them together, and sweeten it with fine powder sugar, then bake it with thin paste under it.

141. *An* ORANGE PUDDING *another Way.*

Take three or four seville oranges, the clearest skins you can get, pare them very thin, boil the peel in a pretty quantity of water, shift them two or three times in the boiling to take out the bitter taste; when it is boiled you must beat it very fine in a marble mortar; take ten eggs, (leave out six of the whites) three quarters of a pound of loaf sugar, beat it and put it to your eggs, beat them together for half an hour, put to them half a pound of melter butter, and the juice of two or three oranges, as they are of goodness, mix all together, and bake it with a thin paste over your dish.

This will make cheese-cakes as well as a pudding.

142. *An* ORANGE PUDDING *another Way.*

Take five or six seville oranges, grate them and make a hole in the top, take out all the meat, and boil the skin very tender, shifting them in the boiling to take off the bitter taste; take half a round of long bisket, slice and scald them with a little cream, beat six eggs and put to your bisket; take half a pound of currans, wash them clean, grate in half a nutmeg, put in a little salt and a glass of sack, beat all together, then put it into your orange skin, tie them tight in a piece of fine cloth, every one separate; about three quarters of an hour will boil them: You must have a little white wine, butter and sugar for sauce.

143. *To make an* ORANGE PIE.

Take half a dozen seville oranges, chip them very fine as you would do for preserving, make a little hole in the top, and scope out all the meat, as you would do an apple, you must boil them whilst they are tender, and shift them two or three times to take off the bitter taste; take six or eight apples, according as they are in bigness, pare and slice them, and put to them part of the pulp of your oranges, and pick out the strings and pippens, put to them half a pound of fine powder sugar, so boil it up over a slow fire, as you would do for puffs, and fill your oranges with it; they must be baked in a deep delf dish with no paste under them; when you put them into your dish put under them three quarters of a pound of fine powder sugar, put in as much water as will wet your sugar, and put your oranges with the open side uppermost; it will take about an hour and half baking in a slow oven; lie over them a light puff-paste; when you dish it up take off the lid, and turn the oranges in the pie, cut the lid in sippets, and set them at an equal distance, to serve it up.

144. *To make a quaking* PUDDING *another Way*.

Take a pint of cream, boil it with one stick of cinnamon, take out the spice when it is boiled, then take the yolks of eight eggs, and four whites, beat them very well with some sack, and mix your eggs with the cream, a little sugar and salt, half a penny wheat loaf, a spoonful of flour, a quarter of a pound of almonds blanch'd and beat fine, beat them altogether, wet a thick cloth, flour it, and put it in when the pot boils; it must boil an hour at least; melted butter, sack and sugar is sauce for it; stick blanch'd almonds and candid orange-peel on the top, so serve it up.

145. *To make* PLUMB PORRIDGE.

Take two shanks of beef, and ten quarts of water, let it boil over a slow fire till it be tender, and when the broth is strong, strain it out, wipe the pot and put in the broth again, slice in two penny loaves thin, cutting off the top and bottom, put some of the liquor to it, cover it up and let it stand for a quarter of an hour, so put it into the pot again, and let it boil a quarter of an hour, then put in four pounds of currans, and let them boil a little; then put in two pounds of raisins, and two pounds of prunes, let them boil till they swell; then put in a quarter of an ounce of mace, a few cloves beat fine, mix it with a little water, and put it into your pot; also a pound of sugar, a little salt, a quart or better of claret, and the juice of two or three lemons or verjuice; thicken it with sagoo instead of bread; so put it in earthen pots, and keep it for use.

146. *To make a* PALPATOON *of* PIGEONS.

Take mushrooms, pallets, oysters and sweet-breads, fry them in butter, put all these in a strong gravy, heat them over the fire, and thicken them up with an egg and a little butter; then take six or eight pigeons, truss them as you would for baking, season them with pepper and salt, and lay on them a crust of forc'd-meat as follows, *viz.* a pound of veal cut in little bits, and a pound and a half of marrow, beat it together in a stone mortar, after it is beat very fine, season it with mace, pepper and salt, put in the yolks of four eggs, and two raw eggs, mix altogether with a few bread crumbs to a paste: make the sides and lid of your pie with it, then put your ragoo into your dish, and lay in your pigeons with butter; an hour and a half will bake it.

147. *To fry* CUCUMBERS *for Mutton Sauce*.

You must brown some butter in a pan, and cut six middling cucumbers, pare and slice them, but not over thin, drain them from the water, then put them into the pan, when they are fried brown put to them a little pepper and salt, a lump of butter, a spoonful of vinegar, a little shred onion, and a little gravy, not to make it too thin, so shake them well together with a little flour.

You may lay them round your mutton, or they are proper for a side-dish.

148. *To force a* FOWL.

Take a good fowl, pull and draw it, then slit the skin down the back, take the flesh from the bones, and mince it very well, mix it with a little beef-suet, shred a jill of large oysters, chop a shalot, a little grated bread, and some sweet herbs, mix all together, season it with nutmeg, pepper and salt, make it up with yolks of eggs, put it on the bones and draw the skin over it, sew up the back, cut off the legs, and put the bones as you do a fowl for boiling, tie the fowl up in a cloth; an hour will boil it. For sauce take a few oysters, shred them, and put them into a little gravy, with a lump of butter, a little lemon-peel shred and a little juice, thicken it up with a little flour, lie the fowl on the dish, and pour the sauce upon it; you may fry a little of the forc'd-meat to lay round. Garnish your dish with lemon; you may set it in the oven if you have convenience, only rub over it the yolk of an egg and a few bread crumbs.

149. *To make* STRAWBERRY *and* RASBERRY FOOL.

Take a pint of rasberries, squeeze and strain the juice, with a spoonful of orange water, put to the juice six ounces of fine sugar, and boil it over the fire; then take a pint of cream and boil it, mix them all well together, and heat them over the fire, but not to boil, if it do it will curdle; stir it till it be cold, put it into your bason and keep it for use.

150. *To make a* POSSET *with* Almonds.

Blanch and beat three quarters of a pound of almonds, so fine that they will spread betwixt your fingers like butter, put in water as you beat them to keep them for oiling; take a pint of sack, cherry or gooseberry wine, and sweeten it to your taste with double refin'd sugar, make it boiling hot; take the almonds, put to them a little water, and boil the wine and almonds together; take the yolks of four eggs, and beat them very well, put to them three or four spoonfuls of wine, then put it into your pan by degrees, stirring it all the while; when it begins to thicken take it off, and stir it a little, put it into a china dish, and serve it up.

151. *To make* DUTCH-BEEF.

Take the lean part of a buttock of beef raw, rub it well with brown sugar all over, and let it lie in a pan or tray two or three hours, turning it three or four times, then salt it with common salt, and two ounces of saltpetre; let it lie a fortnight, turning it every day, then roll it very straight, and put it into a cheese press day and night, then take off the cloth and hang it up to dry in the chimney; when you boil it let it be boiled very well, it will cut in shivers like dutch beef.

You may do a leg of mutton the same way.

152. *To make* PULLONY SAUSAGES.

Take part of a leg of pork or veal, pick it clean from the skin or fat, put to every pound of lean meat a pound of beef-suet, pick'd from the skins, shred the meat and suet separate and very fine, mix them well together, add a large handful of green sage shred very small; season it with pepper and salt, mix it well, press it down hard in an earthen pot, and keep it for use.—When you use them roll them up with as much egg as will make them roll smooth; in rolling them up make them about the length of your fingers, and as thick as two fingers; fry them in butter, which must be boiled before you can put them in, and keep them rolling about in the pan; when they are fried through they are enough.

153. *To make an* AMBLET *of* COCKLES.

Take four whites and two yolks of eggs, a pint of cream, a little flour, a nutmeg grated, a little salt, and a jill of cockles, mix all together, and fry it brown.

This is proper for a side-dish either for noon or night.

154. *To make a common quaking* PUDDING.

Take five eggs, beat them well with a little salt, put in three spoonfuls of fine flour, take a pint of new milk and beat them well together, then take a cloth, butter and flour it, but do not give it over much room in the cloth; an hour will boil it, give it a turn every now and then at the first putting in, or else the meal will settle to the bottom; have a little plain butter for sauce, and serve it up.

155. *To make a boil'd* TANSEY.

Take an old penny loaf, cut off the out crust, slice it thin, put to it as much hot cream as will wet it, six eggs well beaten, a little shred lemon-peel, grate in a little nutmeg, and a little salt; green it as you did your baked tansey, so tie it up in a cloth and boil it; it will take an hour and a quarter boiling; when you dish it up stick it with candid orange and lay a Seville orange cut in quarters round the dish; serve it up with melted butter.

156. *A TANSEY another Way.*

Take an old penny loaf, cut off the out crust, slice it very thin, and put to it as much hot milk as will wet it; take six eggs, beat them very well, grate in half a nutmeg, a little shred lemon-peel, half a pound of clarified butter, half a pound of sugar, and a little salt; mix them well together. *To green your tansey*, Take a handful or two of spinage, a handful of tansey, and a handful or sorrel, clean them and beat them in a marble mortar, or grind it as you would do greensauce, strain it through a linen cloth into a bason, and put into your tansey as much of the juice as will green it, pour over the sauce a little white wine, butter and sugar; lay a rim of paste round your dish and bake it; when you serve it up cut a Seville orange in quarters, and lay it round the edge of the dish.

157. *To make* RICE PANCAKES.

Take half a pound of rice, wash and pick it clean, cree it in fair water till it be a jelly, when it is cold take a pint of cream and the yolks of four eggs, beat them very well together, and put them into the rice, with grated nutmeg and some salt, then put in half a pound of butter, and as much flour as will make it thick enough to fry, with as little butter as you can.

158. *To make* FRUIT FRITTERS.

Take a penny loaf, cut off the out crust, slice it, put to it as much hot milk as will wet it, beat five or six eggs, put to them a quarter of a pound of currans well cleaned, and a little candid orange shred fine, so mix them well together, drop them with a spoon into a stew-pan in clarified butter; have a little white wine, butter and sugar for your sauce, put it into a china bason, lay your fritters round, grate a little sugar over them, and serve them up.

159. *To make* WHITE PUDDINGS *in Skins.*

Take half a pound of rice, cree it in milk while it be soft, when it is creed put it into a cullinder to drain; take a penny loaf, cut off the out crust, then cut it in thin slices, scald it in a little milk, but do not make it over wet; take six eggs and beat them very well, a pound of currans well cleaned, a pound of beef-suet shred fine, two or three spoonfuls of rose-water, half a pound of powder sugar, a little salt, a quarter of an ounce of mace, a large nutmeg grated, and a small stick of cinnamon; beat them together, mix them very well, and put them into the skins; if you find it be too thick put to it a little cream; you may boil them near half an hour, it will make them keep the better.

160. *To make* BLACK PUDDINGS.

Take two quarts of whole oatmeal, pick it and half boil it, give it room in your cloth, (you must do it the day before you use it) put it into the blood while it is warm, with a handful of salt, stir it very well, beat eight or nine eggs in about a pint of cream, and a quart of bread-crumbs, a handful or two of maslin meal dress'd through a hair-sieve, if you have it, if not put in wheat flour; to this quantity you may put an ounce of Jamaica pepper, and ounce of black pepper, a large nutmeg, and a little more salt, sweet-marjoram and thyme, if they be green shred them fine, if dry rub them to powder, mix them well together, and if it be too thick put to it a little milk; take four pounds of beef-suet, and four pounds of lard, skin and cut it it think pieces, put it into your blood by handfuls, as you fill your puddings; when they are filled and tied prick them with a pin, it will keep them from bursting in the boiling; (you must boil them twice) cover them close and it will make them black.

161. *An ORANGE PUDDING another Way.*

Take two Seville oranges, the largest and cleanest you can get, grate off the outer skin with a clean grater; take eight eggs, (leave out two of the whites) half a pound of loaf sugar, beat it very fine, put it to your eggs, and beat them for an hour, put to them half a pound of clarified butter, and four ounces of almonds blanch'd, and heat them with a little rose-water; put in the juice of the oranges, but mind you don't put in the pippens, and mix together; bake it with a thin paste over the bottom of the dish. It must be baked in a slow oven.

162. *To make* APPLE FRITTERS.

Take four eggs and beat them very well, put to them four spoonfuls of fine flour, a little milk, about a quarter of a pound of sugar, a little nutmeg and salt, so beat them very well together; you must not make it very thin, if you do it will not stick to the apple; take a middling apple and pare it, cut out the core, and cut the rest in round slices about the thickness of a shilling; (you may take out the core after you have cut it with your thimble) have ready a little lard in a stew-pan, or any other deep pan; then take your apple every slice single, and dip it into your bladder, let your lard be very hot, so drop them in; you must keep them turning whilst enough, and mind that they be not over brown; as you take them out lay them on a pewter dish before the fire whilst you have done; have a little white wine, butter and sugar for the sauce; grate over them a little loaf sugar, and serve them up.

163. *To make an* HERB PUDDING.

Take a good quantity of spinage and parsley, a little sorrel and mild thyme, put to them a handful of great oatmeal creed, shred them together till they be very small, put to them a pound of currans, well washed and cleaned, four eggs well beaten in a jill of good cream; if you wou'd have it sweet, put in a quarter of a pound of sugar, a little nutmeg, a little salt, and a handful of grated bread; then meal your cloth and tie it close before you put it in to boil; it will take as much boiling as a piece of beef.

164. *To make a* PUDDING *for a* HARE.

Take the liver and chop it small with some thyme, parsley, suet, crumbs of bread mixt, with grated nutmeg, pepper, salt, an egg, a little fat bacon and lemon-peel; you must make the composition very stiff, lest it should dissolve, and you lose your pudding.

165. *To make a* BREAD PUDDING.

Take three jills of milk, when boiled, take a penny loaf sliced thin, cut off the out crust, put on the boiling milk, let it stand close covered till it be cold, and beat it very well till all the lumps be broke; take five eggs beat very well, grate in a little nutmeg, shred some lemon-peel, and a quarter of a pound of butter or beef-suet, with as much sugar as will sweeten it; and currans as many as you please; let them be well cleaned; so put them into your dish, and bake or boil it.

166. *To make* CLARE PANCAKES.

Take five or six eggs, and beat them very well with a little salt, put to them two or three spoonfuls of cream, a spoonful of fine flour, mix it with a little cream; take your clare and wash it very clean, wipe it with a cloth, put your eggs into a pan, just to cover your pan bottom, lay the clare in leaf by leaf, whilst you have covered your pan all over; take a spoon, and pour over every leaf till they are all covered; when it is done lay the brown side upwards, and serve it up.

167. *To make a* LIVER PUDDING.

Take a pound of grated bread, a pound of currans, a pound and a half of marrow and suet together cut small, three quarters of a pound of sugar, half an ounce of cinnamon, a quarter of an ounce of mace, a pint of grated liver, and some salt, mix all together; take twelve eggs, (leave out half of the whites) beat them well, put to them a pint of cream, make the eggs and cream warm, then put it to the pudding, stuff and stir it well together, so fill them in skins; put to them a few blanch'd almonds shred fine, and a spoonful or two of rose-water, so keep them for use.

168. *To make* OATMEAL FRITTERS.

Boil a quart of new milk, steep a pint of fine flour or oatmeal in it ten or twelve hours, then beat four eggs in a little milk, so much as will make like thick blatter, drop them in by spoonfuls into fresh butter, a spoonful of butter in a cake, and grate sugar over them; have sack, butter and sugar for sauce.

169. *To make* APPLE DUMPLINGS.

Take half a dozen codlins, or any other good apples, pare and core them, make a little cold butter paste, and roll it up about the thickness of your finger, so lap around every apple, and tie them single in a fine cloth, boil them in a little salt and water, and let the water boil before you put them in; half an hour will boil them; you must have for sauce a little white wine and butter; grate some sugar round the dish, and serve them up.

170. *To make* HERB DUMPLINGS.

Take a penny loaf, cut off the out crust, and the rest in slices, put to it as much hot milk as will just wet it, take the yolks and whites of six eggs, beat them with two spoonfuls of powder sugar, half a nutmeg, and a little salt, so put it to your bread; take half a pound of currans well cleaned, put them to your eggs, then take a handful of the mildest herbs you can get, gather them so equal that the taste of one be not above the other, wash and chop them very small, put as many of them in as will make a deep green, (don't put any parsley among them, nor any other strong herb) so mix them all together, and boil them in a cloth, make them about the bigness of middling apples; about half an hour will boil them; put them into your dish, and have a little candid orange, white wine, butter and sugar for sauce, so serve them up.

171. *To make* MARROW TARTS.

To a quart of cream put the yolks of twelve eggs, half a pound of sugar, some beaten mace and cinnamon, a little salt and some sack, set it on the fire with half a pound of biskets, as much marrow, a little orange-peel and lemon-peel; stir it on the fire till it becomes thick, and when it is cold put it into a dish with puff-paste, then bake it gently in a slow oven.

172. *To make* PLAIN FRUIT DUMPLINGS.

Take as much flour as you would have dumplings in quantity, put it to a spoonful of sugar, a little salt, a little nutmeg, a spoonful of light yeast, and half a pound of currans well washed and cleaned, so knead them the stiffness you do a common dumpling, you must have white wine, sugar and butter for sauce; you may boil them either in a cloth or without; so serve them up.

173. *To make* OYSTER LOAVES.

Take half a dozen French loaves, rasp them and make a hole at the top, take out all the crumbs and fry them in butter till they be crisp; when your oysters are stewed, put them into your loaves, cover them up before the fire to keep hot whilst you want them; so serve them up.

They are proper either for a side-dish or mid-dish.

You may make cockle loaves or mushroom-loaves the same way.

174. *To make a* GOOSEBERRY PUDDING.

Take a quart of green gooseberries, pick, coddle, bruise and rub them through a hair-sieve to take out the pulp; take six spoonfuls of the pulp, six eggs, three quarters of a pound of sugar, half a pound of clarified butter, a little lemon-peel shred fine, a handful of bread-crumbs or bisket, a spoonful of rose-water or orange-flower water; mix these well together, and bake it with paste round the dish; you may add sweet-meats if you please.

175. *To make an* EEL PIE.

Case and clean the eels, season them with a little nutmeg, pepper and salt, cut them in long pieces; you must make your pie with hot butter paste, let it be oval with a thin crust; lay in your eels length way, putting over them a little fresh butter; so bake them.

Eel pies are good, and eat very well with currans, but if you put in currans you must not use any black pepper, but a little Jamaica pepper.

176. *To make a* TURBOT-HEAD PIE.

Take a middling turbot-head, pretty well cut off, wash it clean, take out the gills, season it pretty well with mace, pepper and salt, so put it into a deep dish with half a pound of butter, cover it with a light puff-paste, but lay none in the bottom; when it is baked take out the liquor and the butter that it was baked in, put it into a sauce-pan with a lump of fresh butter and flour to thicken it, with an anchovy and a glass of white wine, so pour it into your pie again over the fish; you may lie round half a dozen yolks of eggs at an equal distance; when you have cut off the lid, lie it in sippets round your disk, and serve it up.

177. *To make a Caudle for a sweet* VEAL PIE.

Take about a jill of white wine and verjuice mixed, make it very hot, beat the yolk of an egg very well, and then mix them together as you would do mull'd ale; you must sweeten it very well, because there is no sugar in the pie.

This caudle will do for any other sort of pie that is sweet.

178. *To make* SWEET-MEAT TARTS.

Make a little shell-paste, roll it, and line your tins, prick them in the inside, and so bake them; when you serve 'em up put in any sort of sweet-meats, what you please.

You may have a different sort every day, do but keep your shells bak'd by you.

179. *To make* ORANGE TARTS.

Take two or three Seville oranges and boil them, shift them in the boiling to take out the bitter, cut them in two, take out the pippens, and cut them in slices; they must be baked in crisp paste; when you fill the petty-pans, lay in a layer of oranges and a layer of sugar, (a pound will sweeten a dozen of small tins, if you do not put in too much orange) bake them in a slow oven, and ice them over.

180. *To make a* TANSEY *another Way.*

Take a pint of cream, some biskets without seeds, two or three spoonfuls of fine flour, nine eggs, leaving out two of the whites, some nutmeg, and orange-flower water, a little juice of tansey and spinage, put it into a pan till it be pretty thick, then fry or bake it, if fried take care that you do not let it be over-brown. Garnish with orange and sugar, so serve it up.

181. *A good* PASTE *for* TARTS.

Take a pint of flour, and rub a quarter of a pound of butter into it, beat two eggs with a spoonful of double-refin'd sugar, and two or three spoonfuls of cream to make it into paste; work it as little as you can, roll it out thin; butter your tins, dust on some flour, then lay in your paste, and do not fill them too full.

182. *To make* TRANSPARENT TARTS.

Take a pound of flour well dried, beat one egg till it be very thin, then melt almost three quarters of a pound of butter without salt, and let it be cold enough to mix with an egg, then put it into the flour and make your paste, roll it very thin, when you are setting them into the oven wet them over with a little fair water, and grate a little sugar; if you bake them rightly they will be very nice.

183. *To make a* SHELL PASTE.

Take half a pound of fine flour, and a quarter of a pound of butter, the yolks of two eggs and one white, two ounces of sugar finely sifted, mix all these together with a little water, and roll it very thin whilst you can see through it; when you lid your tarts prick them to keep them from blistering; make sure to roll them even, and when you bake them ice them.

184. *To make* PASTE *for* TARTS.

Take the yolks of five or six eggs, just as you would have paste in quantity; to the yolks of eggs put a pound of butter, work the butter with your hands whilst it take up all the eggs, then take some London flour and work it with your butter whilst it comes to a paste, put in about two spoonfuls of loaf sugar beat and sifted, and about half a jill of water; when you have wrought it well together it is fit for use.

This is a paste that seldom runs if it be even roll'd; roll it thin but let your lids be thiner than your bottoms; when you have made your tarts, prick them over with a pin to keep it from blistering; when you are going to put them into the oven, wet them over with a feather dipt in fair water, and grate over them a little double-refined loaf sugar, it will ice them; but don't let them be bak'd in a hot oven.

185. *A short* PASTE *for* TARTS.

Take a pound of wheat-flour, and rub it very small, three quarters of a pound of butter, rub it as small as the flour, put to it three spoonfuls of loaf sugar beat and sifted; take the yolks of four eggs, and beat them very well; put to them a spoonful or two of rose-water, and work them into a paste, then roll them thin, and ice them as you did the other if you please, and bake 'em in a slow oven.

186. *To make a* LIGHT PASTE *for a* VENISON PASTY, *or other* PIE.

Take a quarter of a peck of fine flour, or as much as you think you have occasion for, and to every quartern of flour put a pound and a quarter of butter, break the third part of your butter into the flour; then take the whites of three or four eggs, beat them very well to a froth, and put to them as much water as will knead the meal; do not knead it over stiff, so then roll it in the rest of your butter; you must roll it five or six times over at least, and strinkle a little flour over your butter every time you roll it up, lap it up the cross way, and it will be fit for use.

187. *To make a Paste for a* STANDING PIE.

Take a quartern of flour or more if you have occasion, and to every quartern of flour put a pound of butter, and a little salt, knead it with boiling water, then work it very well, and let it lie whilst it is cold.

This paste is good enough for a goose pie, or any other standing-pie.

188. *A light Paste for a* DISH PIE.

Take a quartern of flour, and break into it a pound of butter in large pieces, knead it very stiff, handle it as lightly as you can, and roll it once or twice, then it is fit for use.

189. *To make* CHEESE CAKES.

Take a gallon of new milk, make of it a tender curd, wring the whey from it, put it into a bason, and break three quarters of a pound of butter into the curd, then with a clean hand work the butter and curd together till all the butter be melted, and rub it in a hair-sieve with the back of spoon till all be through; then take six eggs, beat them with a few spoonfuls of rose-water or sack, put it into your curd with half a pound of fine sugar and a nutmeg grated; mix them all together with a little salt, some currans and almonds; then make up your paste of fine flour, with cold butter and a little sugar; roll your paste very thin, fill your tins with the curd, and set them in an oven, when they are almost enough take them out, then take a quarter of a pound of butter, with a little rose-water, and part of a half pound of sugar, let it stand on the coals till the butter be melted, then pour into each cake some of it, set them in the oven again till they be brown, so keep them for use.

190. *To make* GOOFER WAFERS.

Take a pound of fine flour and six eggs, beat them very well, put to them about a jill of milk, mix it well with the flour, put in half a pound of clarified butter, half a pound of powder sugar, half of a nutmeg, and a little salt; you may add to it two or three spoonfuls of cream; then take your goofer-irons and put them into the fire to heat, when they are hot rub them over the first time with a little butter in a cloth, put your batter into one side of your goofer-irons, put them into the fire, and keep turning the irons every now and then; (if your irons be too hot they burn soon) make them a day or two before you use them, only set them down before the fire on a pewter dish before you serve them up; have a little white wine and butter for your sauce, grating some sugar over them.

191. *To make common* CURD CHEESE CAKES.

Take a pennyworth of curds, mix them with a little cream, beat four eggs, put to them six ounces of clarified butter, a quarter of a pound of sugar, half a pound of currans well wash'd, and a little lemon-peel shred, a little nutmeg, a spoonful of rose-water or brandy, whether you please, and a little salt, mix altogether, and bake them in small petty pans.

192. CHEESE CAKES *without* CURRANS.

Take five quarts of new milk, run it to a tender curd, then hang it in a cloth to drain, rub into them a pound of butter that is well washed in rose-water, put to it the yolks of seven or eight eggs, and two of the whites; season it with cinnamon, nutmeg and sugar.

193. *To make a* CURD PUDDING.

Take three quarts of new milk, put to it a little erning, as much as will break it when it is scumm'd break it down with your hand, and when it is drained grind it with a mustard ball in a bowl, or beat it in a marble-mortar; then take half a pound of butter and six eggs, leaving out three of the whites; beat the eggs well, and put them into the curds and butter, grate in half a nutmeg, a little lemon-peel shred fine, and salt, sweeten it to your taste, beat them all together, and bake them in little petty-pans with fast bottoms; a quarter of an hour will bake them; you must butter the tins very well before you put them in; when you dish them up you must lay them the wrong side upwards on the dish, and stick them with either blanch'd almonds, candid orange, or citron cut in long bits, and grate a little loaf sugar over them.

194. *To make a* SLIPCOAT CHEESE.

Take five quarts of new-milk, a quart of cream, and a quart of water, boil your water, then put your cream to it; when your milk is new-milk warm put in your erning, take your curd into the strainer, break it as little as you can, and let it drain, then put it into your vat, press it by degrees, and lay it in grass.

195. *To make* CREAM CHEESE.

Take three quarts of new-milk, one quart of cream, and a spoonful of erning, put them together, let it stand till it come to the hardness of a strong jelly, then put it into the mould, shifting it often into dry cloths, lay the weight of three pounds upon it, and about two hours after you may lay six or seven pounds upon it; turn it often into dry cloths till night, then take the weight off, and let it lie in the mould without weight and cloth till morning, and when it is so dry that it doth not wet a cloth, keep it in greens till fit for use; if you please you may put a little salt into it.

196. *To make* PIKE *eat like* STURGEON.

Take the thick part of a large pike and scale it, set on two quarts of water to boil it in, put in a jill of vinegar, a large handful of salt, and when it boils put in your pike, but first bind it about with coarse inkle; when it is boiled you must not take off the inkle or baising, but let it be on all the time it is in eating; it must be kept in the same pickle it was boiled in, and if you think it be not strong enough you must add a little more salt and vinegar, so when it is cold put it upon your pike, and keep it for use; before you boil the pike take out the bone.

You may do scate the same way, and in my opinion it eats more like sturgeon.

197. *To Collar* EELS.

Take the largest eels you can get, skin and split them down the belly, take out the bones, season them with a little mace, nutmeg and salt; begin at the tail and roll them up very tight, so bind them up in a little coarse inkle, boil it in salt and water, a few bay leaves, a little whole pepper, and a little alegar or vinegar; it will take an hour boiling, according as your roll is in bigness; when it is boiled you must tie it and hang it up whilst it be cold, then put it into the liquor that it was boiled in, and keep it for use.

If your eels be small you may robe two or three of them together.

198. *To Pot* SMELTS.

Take the freshest and largest smelts you can get, wipe them very well with a clean cloth, take out the guts with a skewer, (but you must not take out the milt and roan) season them with a little mace, nutmeg and salt, so lie them in a flat pot; if you have two score you must lay over them five ounces of butter; lie over them a paper, and set them in a slow oven; if it be over hot it will burn them, and make them look black; an hour will bake them; when they are baked you must take them out and lay them on a dish to drain, and when they are drained you must put them in long pots about the length of your smelts; when you lay them in you must put betwixt every layer the same seasoning as you did before, to make them keep; when they are cold cover them over with clarified butter, so keep them for use.

199. *To Pickle* SMELTS.

Take the best and largest smelts you can get; gut, wash and wipe them, lie them in a flat pot, cover them with a little white wine vinegar, two or three blades of mace and a little pepper and salt; bake them in a slow oven, and keep them for use.

200. *To stew a* PIKE.

Take a large pike, scale and clean it, season it in the belly with a little mace and salt; skewer it round, put it into a deep stew-pan, with a pint of small gravy and a pint of claret, two or thee blades of mace, set it over a stove with a slow fire, and cover it up close; when it is enough take part of the liquor, put to it two anchovies, a little lemon-peel shred fine, and thicken the sauce with flour and butter; before you lie the pike on the dish turn it with the back upwards, take off the skin, and serve it up. Garnish your dish with lemon and pickle.

201. SAUCE *for a* PIKE.

Take a little of the liquor that comes from the pike when you take it out of the oven, put to it two or three anchovies, a little lemon-peel shred, a spoonful or two of white wine, or a little juice of lemon, which you please, put to it some butter and flour, make your sauce about the thickness of cream, put it into a bason or silver-boat, and set in your dish with your pike, you may lay round your pike any sort of fried fish, or broiled, if you have it; you may have the same sauce for a broiled pike, only add a little good gravy, a few shred capers, a little parsley, and a spoonful or two of oyster and cockle pickle if you have it.

202. *How to roast a* PIKE *with a Pudding in the Belly.*

Take a large pike, scale and clean it, draw it at the gills.—*To make a pudding for the Pike.* Take a large handful of bread-crumbs, as much beef-suet shred fine, two eggs, a little pepper and salt, a little grated nutmeg, a little parsley, sweet-marjoram and lemon-peel shred fine; so mix altogether, put it into the belly of your pike, skewer it round and lie it in an earthen dish with a lump of butter over it, a little salt and flour, so set it in the oven; an hour will roast it.

203. *To dress a* COD'S HEAD.

Take a cod's head, wash and clean it, take out the gills, cut it open, and make it to lie flat; (if you have no conveniency of boiling it you may do it in an oven, and it will be as well or better) put it into a copper-dish or earthen one, lie upon it a littler butter, salt, and flour, and when it is enough take off the skin.

SAUCE *for the* COD'S HEAD.

Take a little white gravy, about a pint of oysters or cockles, a little shred lemon-peel, two or three spoonfuls of white wine, and about half a pound of butter thicken'd with flour, and put it into your boat or bason.

Another SAUCE *for a* COD'S HEAD.

Take a pint of good gravy, a lobster or crab, which you can get, dress and put it into your gravy with a little butter, juice of lemon, shred lemon-peel, and a few shrimps if you have them; thicken it with a little flour, and put it into your bason, set the oysters on one side of the dish and this on the other; lay round the head boiled whitings, or any fried fish; pour over the head a little melted butter. Garnish your dish with horse-radish, slices of lemon and pickles.

204. *To stew* CARP *or* TENCH.

Take your carp or tench and wash them, scale the carp but not the tench, when you have cleaned them wipe them with a cloth, and fry them in a frying pan with a little butter to harden the skin; before you put them into the stew-pan, put to them a little good gravy, the quantity will be according to the largeness of your fish, with a jill of claret, three or four anchovies at least, a little shred lemon-peel, a blade or two of mace, let all stew together, till your carp be enough, over a slow fire; when it is enough take part of the liquor, put to it half a pound of butter, and thicken it with a little flour; so serve them up. Garnish your dish with crisp parsley, slices of lemon and pickles.

If you have not the convenience of stewing them, you may broil them before a fire, only adding the same sauce.

205. *How to make* SAUCE *for a boiled* SALMON *or* TURBOT.

Take a little mild white gravy, two or three anchovies, a spoonful of oyster or cockle pickle, a little shred lemon-peel, half a pound of butter, a little parsley and fennel shred small, and a little juice of lemon, but not too much, for fear it should take off the sweetness.

206. *To make* SAUCE *for* HADDOCK *or* COD, *either broiled or boiled.*

Take a little gravy, a few cockles,

oysters or mushrooms, put to them a little of the gravy that comes from the fish, either broiled or boiled, it will do very well if you have no other gravy, a little catchup and a lump of butter; if you have neither oysters nor cockles you may put in an anchovy or two, and thicken with flour; you may put in a few shred capers, or a little mango, if you have it.

207. *To stew* EELS.

Take your eels, case, clean and skewer them round, put them into a stew-pan with a little good gravy, a little claret to redden the gravy, a blade or two of mace, an anchovy, and a little lemon-peel; when they are enough thicken them with a little flour and butter. Garnish your dish with parsley.

208. *To pitch-cock* EELS.

Take your eels, case and clean them, season them with nutmeg, pepper and salt, skewer them round, broil them before the fire, and baste them with a little butter; when they are almost enough strinkle them over with a little shred parsley, and make your sauce of a little gravy, butter, anchovy, and a little oyster pickle if you have it; don't pour the sauce over your eels, put it into a china bason, and set it in the middle of your dish.

Garnish with crisp parsley, and serve them up.

209. *To boil* HERRINGS.

Take your herring, scale and wash them, take out the milt and roan, skewer them round, and tie them with a string or else they will come loose in the boiling and be spoil'd; set on a pretty broad stew-pan, with as much water as will cover them, put to it a little salt, lie in you herrings with the backs downwards boil with them the milt and roans to lie round them; they will boil in half a quarter of an hour over a slow fire; when they are boiled take them up with an egg slice, so turn them over and set them to drain. Make your sauce of a little gravy and butter, an anchovy and a little boiled parsley shred; put it into the bason, set it in the middle of the dish, lie the herrings round with their tails towards the bason, and lie the milts and roans between every herring. Garnish with crisp parsley and lemon; so serve them up.

210. *To fry* HERRINGS.

Scale and wash your herrings clean, strew over them a little flour and salt; let your butter be very hot before you put your herrings into the pan, then shake them to keep them stirring, and fry them over a brisk fire; when they are fried cut off the heads and bruise them, put to them a jill of ale, (but the ale must not be bitter) add a little pepper and salt, a small onion or shalot, if you have them, and boil them altogether; when they are boiled, strain them, and put them into your sauce-pan again, thicken them with a little flour and butter, put it into a bason, and set it in the middle of your dish; fry the milts and roans together, and lay round your herrings. Garnish your dish with crisp parsley, and serve it up.

211. *To pickle* HERRINGS.

Scale and clean your herrings, take out the milts and roans, and skewer them round, season them with a little pepper and salt, put them in a deep pot, cover them with alegar, put to them a little whole Jamaica pepper, and two or three bay leaves; bake them and keep them for use.

212. *To stew* OYSTERS.

Take a score or two of oysters, according as you have occasion, put them into a small stew-pan, with a few bread-crumbs, a little water, shred mace and pepper, a lump of butter, and a spoonful of vinegar, (not to make it four) boil them altogether but not over much, if you do it makes them hard. Garnish with bread fippets, and serve them up.

213. *To fry* OYSTERS.

Take a score or two of the largest oysters you can get, and the yolks of four or five eggs, beat them very well, put to them a little nutmeg, pepper and salt, a spoonful of fine flour, and a little raw parsley shred, so dip in your oysters, and fry them in butter a light brown.

They are very proper to lie about either stew'd oysters, or any other fish, or made dishes.

214. OYSTERS *in* SCALLOP SHELLS.

Take half a dozen small scallop shells, lay in the bottom of every shell a lump of butter, a few bread crumbs, and then your oysters; laying over them again a few more bread crumbs, a little butter, and a little beat pepper, so set them to crisp, either in the oven or before the fire, and serve them up.

They are proper for either a side-dish or middle-dish.

215 *To keep* HERRINGS *all the Year*.

Take fresh herrings, cut off their heads, open and wash them very clean, season them with salt, black pepper, and Jamaica pepper, put them into a pot, cover them with white wine vinegar and water, of each an equal quantity, and set them in a slow oven to bake; tie the pot up close and they will keep a year in the pickle.

216. *To make artificial* Sturgeon *another Way*.

Take out the bones of a turbot or britt, lay it in salt twenty four hours, boil it with good store of salt; make your pickle of white wine vinegar and three quarts of water, boil them, and put in a little vinegar in the boiling; don't boil it over much, if you do it will make it soft; when 'tis enough take it out till it be cold, put the same pickle to it, and keep it for use.

217. *To stew* MUSHROOMS.

Take mushrooms, and clean them, the buttons you may wash, but the flaps you must pill both inside and out; when you have cleaned them, pick out the little ones for pickling, and cut the rest in pieces for stewing; wash them and put them into a little water, give them a boil and it will take off the faintness, so drain from them all the water, then put them into a pan with a lump of butter, a little shred mace, pepper and salt to your taste (putting them to a little water) hang them over a slow fire for half an hour, when they are enough thicken them with a little flour; serve them up with sippets.

218. *To make* ALMOND PUFFS.

Take a pound of almonds blanch'd, and beat them with orange-flower water, then take a pound of sugar, and boil them almost to a candy height, put in your almonds and stir them on the fire, keep them stirring till they be stiff, then take them off the fire and stir them till they be cold; beat them a quarter of an hour in a mortar, putting to them a pound of sugar sifted, and a little lemon-peel grated, make it into a paste with the whites of three eggs, and beat it into a froth more or less as you think proper; bake them in an oven almost cold, and keep them for use.

219. *To pot* MUSHROOMS.

Take the largest mushrooms, scrape and clean them, put them into your pan with a lump of butter, and a little salt, let then stew over a slow fire whilst they are enough, put to them a little mace and whole pepper, then dry them with a cloth, and put them down into a pot as close as you can, and as you lie them down strinkle in a little salt and mace, when they are cold cover them over with butter; when you use them toss them up with gravy, a few bread-crumbs and butter; do not make your pot over large, but rather put them into two pots; they will keep the better if you take the gravy from them when they are stewed.

They are good for fish-sauce, or any other whilst they are fresh.

220. *To fry* TROUT, *or any other Sort of Fish.*

Take two or three eggs, more or less according as you have fish to fry, take the fish and cut it in thin slices, lie it upon a board, rub the eggs over it with a feather, and strow on a little flour and salt, fry it in fine drippings or butter, let the drippings be very hot before you put in the fish, but do not let it burn, if you do it will make the fish black; when the fish is in the pan, you may do the other side with the egg, and as you fry it lay it to drain before the fire till all be fried, then it is ready for use.

221. *To make* SAUCE *for* SALMON *or* TURBOT.

Boil your turbot or salmon, and set it to drain; take the gravy that drains from the salmon or turbot, an anchovy or two, a little lemon-peel shred, a spoonful of catchup, and a little butter, thicken it with flour the thickness of cream, put to it a little shred parsley and fennel; but do not put in your parsley and fennel till you be just going to send it up, for it will take off the green.

The gravy of all sorts of fish is a great addition to your sauce, if the fish be sweet.

222. *To dress* COD'S ZOONS.

Lie them in water all night, and then boil them, if they be salt shift them once in the boiling, when they are tender cut them in long pieces, dress them up with eggs as you do salt fish, take one or two of them and cut into square pieces, dip them in egg and fry them to lay round your dish.

It is proper to lie about any other dish.

223. *To make* SOLOMON GUNDY *to eat in Lent*

Take five or six white herrings, lay them in water all night, boil them as soft as you would do for eating, and shift them in the boiling to take out the saltness; when they are boiled take the fish from the bone, and mind you don't break the bone in pieces, leaving on the head and tail; take the white part of the herrings, a quarter of a pound of anchovies, a large apple, a little onion shred fine, or shalot, and a little lemon-peel, shred them all together, and lie them over the bones on both sides, in the shape of a herring; then take off the peel of a lemon very very thin, and cut it in long bits, just as it will reach over the herrings; you must lie this peel over every herring pretty thick. Garnish your dish with a few pickled oysters, capers, and mushrooms, if you have any; so serve them up.

224. SOLOMAN GUNDY *another Way.*

Take the white part of a turkey, or other fowl, if you have neither, take a little white veal and mince it pretty small; take a little hang beef or tongues, scrape them very fine, a few shred capers, and the yolks of four or five eggs shred small; take a delf dish and lie a delf plate in the dish with the wrong side up, so lie on your meat and other ingredients, all single in quarters, one to answer another; set in the middle a large lemon or mango, so lie round your dish anchovies in lumps, picked oysters or cockles, and a few pickled mushrooms, slices of lemon and capers; so serve it up.

This is proper for a side-dish either at noon or night.

225. *To make* LEMON CHEESE CAKES.

Blanch half a pound of almonds, and beat them in a stone mortar very fine, with a little rose-water; put in eight eggs, leaving out five of the whites; take three quarters of a pound of sugar, and three quarters of a pound of melted butter, beat all together, then take three lemon-skins, boiled tender, the rind and all, beat them very well, and mix them with the rest, then put them into your paste.

You may make a lemon-pudding the same way, only add the juice of half a lemon: Before you set them in the oven, grate over them a little fine loaf sugar.

226. *To make white* GINGER BREAD.

Take a little gum-dragon, lay it in rose-water all night, then take a pound of jordan almonds blanch'd with a little of the gum-water, a pound of double-refined sugar beat and sifted, an ounce of cinnamon beat with a little rose-water, work it into a paste and print it, then set it in a stove to dry.

227. *To make red* GINGER BREAD.

Take a quart and a jill of red wine, a jill and a half of brandy, seven or eight manshets, according to the size the bread is, grate them, (the crust must be dried, beat and sifted) three pounds and a half of sugar beat and sifted, two ounces of cinnamon, and two ounces of ginger beat and sifted, a pound of almonds blanched and beat with rose-water, put the bread into the liquor by degrees, stirring it all the time, when the bread is all well mix'd take it off the fire; you must put the sugar, spices, and almonds into it, when it is cold print it; keep some of the spice to dust the prints with.

228. *To make a* GREAT CAKE.

Take five pounds of fine flour, (let it be dried very well before the fire) and six pounds of currans well dress'd and rub'd in cloths after they are wash'd, set them in a sieve before the fire; you must weigh your currans after they are cleaned, then take three quarters of an ounce of mace, two large nutmegs beaten and mix'd amongst the flour, and pound of powder sugar, and pound of citron, and a pound of candid orange, (cut your citron and orange in pretty large pieces) and a pound of almonds cut in three or four pieces long way; then take sixteen eggs, leaving out half of the whites, beat your sugar and eggs for half an hour with a little salt; take three jills of cream, and three pounds and a half of butter, melt your butter with part of the cream for fear it should be too hot, put in between a jack and a jill of good brandy, a quart of light yeast, and the rest of the cream, mix all your liquors together about blood-warm, make a hole in the middle of your flour, and put in the liquids, cover it half an hour and let it stand to rise, then put in your currans and mix all together; butter your hoop, tie a paper three fold, and put it at the bottom in your hoop; just when they are ready to set in the oven, put the cake into your hoop at three times; when you have laid a little paste at the bottom, lay in part of your sweet-meats and almonds, then put in a little paste over them again, and the rest of your sweet-meats and almonds, and set it in a quick oven; two hours will bake it.

229. *To make* ICEING *for this* CAKE.

Take two pounds of double-refined sugar, beat it, and sift it through a fine sieve; put to it a spoonful of fine starch, a pennyworth of gum-arabic, beat them all well together; take the whites of four or five eggs, beat them well, and put to them a spoonful of rose-water, or orange-flower water, a spoonful of the juice of lemon, beat them with the whites of your eggs, and put in a little to your sugar till you wet it, then beat them for two hours whilst your cake is baking; if you make it over thin it will run; when you lie it on your cake you must lie it on with a knife; if you would have the iceing very thick, you must add a little more sugar; wipe off the loose currans before you put on the iceing, and put it into the oven to harden the iceing.

230. *To make a* PLUMB CAKE.

Take five pounds of flour dried and cold, mix to it an ounce of mace, half an ounce of cinnamon, a quarter of an ounce of nutmegs, half a quarter of an ounce of lemon-peel grated, and a pound of fine sugar; take fifteen eggs, leaving out seven of the whites, beat your eggs with half a jill of brandy or sack, a little orange-flower water, or rose water; then put to your eggs near a quart of light yeast, set it on the fire with a quart of cream, and three pounds of butter, let your butter melt in the cream, so let it stand till new milk warm, then skim off all the butter and most of the milk, and mix it to your eggs and yeast; make a hole in the middle of your flour, and put in your yeast, strinkle at the tip a little flour, then mix to it a little salt, six pounds of currans well wash'd clean'd, dry'd, pick'd, and plump'd by the fire, a pound of the best raisins stoned, and beat them altogether whilst they leave the bowl; put in a pound of candid orange, and half a pound of citron cut in long pieces; then butter the garth and fill it full; bake it in a quick oven, against it be enough have an iceing ready.

231. *To make a* CARRAWAY CAKE.

Take eighteen eggs, leave out half of the whites, and beat them; take two pounds of butter, wash the butter clear from milk and salt, put to it a little rose-water, and wash your butter very well with your hands till it take up all the eggs, then mix them in half a jack of brandy and sack; grate into your eggs a lemon rind; put in by degrees (a spoonful at a time) two pounds of fine flour, a pound and a half of loaf sugar, that is sifted and dry; when you have mixed them very well with your hands, take a thible and beat it very well for half an hour, till it look very white, then mix to it a few seeds, six ounces of carraway comfits, and half a pound of citron and candid orange; then beat it well, butter your garth, and put it in a quick oven.

232. *To make* CAKES *to keep all the Year.*

Have in readiness a pound and four ounces of flour well dried, take a pound of butter unsalted, work it with a pound of white sugar till it cream, three spoonfuls of sack, and the rind of an orange, boil it till it is not bitter, and beat it with sugar, work these together, then clean your hands, and grate a nutmeg into your flour, put in three eggs and two whites, mix them well, then with a paste-pin or thible stir in your flour to the butter, make them up into little cakes, wet the top with sack and strow on fine sugar; bake them on buttered papers, well floured, but not too much; you may add a pound of currans washed and warmed.

233. *To make* SHREWSBERRY CAKES.

Take two pounds of fine flour, put to it a pound and a quarter of butter (rub them very well) a pound and a quarter of fine sugar sifted, grate in a nutmeg, beat in three whites of eggs and two yolks, with a little rose-water, and so knead your paste with it, let it lay an hour, then make it up into cakes, prick them and lay them on papers, wet them with a feather dipt in rose-water, and grate over them a little fine sugar; bake them in a slow oven, either on tins or paper.

234. *To make a fine* CAKE.

Take five pounds of fine flour dried, and keep it warm; four pounds of loaf sugar pounded, sifted and warmed; five pounds of currans well cleaned and warmed before the fire; a pound and a half of almonds blanch'd beat, dried, slit and kept warm; five pounds of good butter well wash'd and beat from the water; then work it an hour and a half till it comes to a fine cream; put to the butter all the sugar, work it up, and then the flour, put in a pint of brandy, then all the whites and yolks of the eggs, mix all the currans and almonds with the rest. There must be four pounds of eggs in weight in the shells, the yolks and the whites beat and separated, the whites beat to a froth; you must not cease beating till they are beat to a curd, to prevent oiling; to the quantity of a cake put a pound and a half of orange-peel and citron shred, without plumbs, and half a pound of carraway seeds, it will require four hours baking, and the oven must be as hot as for bread, but let it be well slaked when it has remained an hour in the oven, and stop it close; you may ice it if you please.

235. *To make a* SEED CAKE.

Take one quartern of fine flour well dried before the fire, when it is cold rub in a pound of butter; take three quarters of a pound of carraway comfits, six spoonfuls of new yeast, six spoonfuls of cream, the yolks of six eggs and two whites, and a little sack; mix all of these together in a very light paste, set it before the fire till it rise, and so bake it in a tin.

236. *To make an ordinary* PLUMB CAKE.

Take a pound of flour well dried before the fire, a pound of currans, two penny-worth of mace and cloves, two eggs, four spoonfuls of good new yeast, half a pound of butter, half a pint of cream, melt the butter, warm the cream, and mix altogether in a very light paste, butter your tin before you put it in; an hour will bake it.

237. *To make an* ANGELICA CAKE.

Take the stalks of angelica boil and green them very well, put to every pound of pulp a pound of loaf sugar beaten very well, and when you think it is beaten enough, lay them in what fashion you please on glasses, and as they candy turn them.

238. *To make* KING CAKES.

Take a pound of flour, three quarters of a pound of butter, half a pound of sugar and half a pound of currans, well cleaned; rub your butter well into your flour, and put in as many yolks of eggs as will lithe them, then put in your sugar, currans, and some mace, shred in as much as will give them a taste, so make them up in little round cakes, and butter the papers you lie them on.

239. *To make* BREAKFAST CAKES.

Take a pound of currans well washed, (rub them in a cloth till dry) a pound of flour dried before a fire, take three eggs, leave out one of the whites, four spoonfuls of new yeast, and four spoonfuls of sack or two of brandy, beat the yeast and eggs well together; then take a jill of cream, and something above a quarter of a pound of butter, set them on a fire, and stir them till the butter be melted, (but do not let them boil) grate a large nutmeg into the flour, with currans and five spoonfuls of sugar; mix all together, beat it with your hand till it leave the bowl, then flour the tins you put the paste in, and let them stand a little to rise, then bake them an hour and a quarter.

240. *To make* MACCAROONS.

Take a pound of blanched almonds and beat them, put some rose-water in while beating; (they must not be beaten too small) mix them with the whites of five eggs, a pound of sugar finely beaten and sifted, and a handful of flour, mix all these very well together, lay them on wafers, and bake them in a very temperate oven, (it must not be so hot as for manchet) then they are fit for use.

241. *To make* WHIGGS.

Take two pounds of flour, a pound of butter, a pint of cream, four eggs, (leaving out two of the whites) and two spoonfuls of yeast, set them to rise a little; when they are mixed add half a pound of sugar, and half a pound of carraway comfits, make them up with sugar and bake them in a dripping pan.

242. *To make* RASBERRY CREAM.

Take rasberries, bruise them, put 'em in a pan on a quick fire whilst the juice be dried up, then take the same weight of sugar as you have rasberries, and set them on a slow fire, let them boil whilst they are pretty stiff; make them into cakes, and dry them near the fire or in the sun.

243. *To make* QUEEN CAKES.

Take a pound of London flour dry'd well before the fire, nine eggs, a pound of loaf sugar beaten and sifted, put one half to your eggs and the other to your butter; take a pound of butter and melt it without water put it into a stone bowl, when it is almost cold put in your sugar and a spoonful or two of rose water, beat it very quick, for half an hour, till it be as white as cream; beat the eggs and sugar as long and very quick, whilst they be white; when they are well beat mix them all together; then take half a pound of currans cleaned well, and a little shred of mace, so you may fill one part of your tins before you put in your currans; you may put a quarter of a pound of almonds shred (if you please) into them that is without currans; you may ice them if you please, but do not let the iceing be thicker than you may lie on with a little brush.

244. *To make a* BISKET CAKE.

Take a pound of London flour dry'd before the fire, a pound of loaf sugar beaten and sifted, beat nine eggs and a spoonful or two of rose water with the sugar for two hours, then put them to your flour and mix them well together; put in an ounce of carraway seeds, then put it into your tin and bake it an hour and a half in a pretty quick oven.

245. *To make* CRACKNELS.

Take half a pound of fine flour, half a pound of sugar, two ounces of butter, two eggs, and a few carraway seeds; (you must beat and sift the sugar) then put it to your flour and work it to paste; roll them as thin as you can, and cut them out with queen cake tins, lie them on papers and bake them in a slow oven.

They are proper to eat with chocolate.

246. *To make* PORTUGAL CAKES.

Take a pound of flour, a pound of butter, a pound of sugar, a pound of currans well cleaned, and a nutmeg grated; take half of the flour and mix it with sugar and nutmeg, melt the butter and put it into the yolks of eight eggs very well beat, and only four of the whites, and as the froth rises put it into the flour, and do so till all is in; then beat it together, still strowing some of the other half of the flour, and then beat it till all the flour be in, then butter the pans and fill them, but do not bake them too much; you may ice them if you please, or you may strow carraway comfits of all sorts on them when they go into the oven. The currans must be plump'd in warm water, and dried before the fire, then put them into your cakes.

247. *To make* PLUMB-CAKES *another way*.

Take two pounds of butter, beat it with a little rose water and orange-flower water till it be like cream, two pounds of flour dried before the fire, a quarter of an ounce of mace, a nutmeg, half a pound of loaf sugar, beat and sifted, fifteen eggs (beat the whites by themselves and yolks with your sugar) a jack of brandy and as much sack, two pounds of currans very well cleaned, and half a pound of almonds blanch'd and cut in two or three pieces length-way, so mix all together, and put it into your hoop of tin; you may put in half a pound of candid orange and citron if you please; about an hour will bake it in a quick oven; if you have a mind to have it iced a pound of sugar will ice it.

248. *To make a* GINGER BREAD-CAKE.

Take two pounds of treacle, two pounds and a quartern of flour, and ounce of beat ginger, three quarters of a pound of sugar, two ounces of coriander seeds, two eggs, a pennyworth of new ale with the yeast on it, a glass of brandy, and two ounces of lemon-peel, mix all these together in a bowl, and set it to rise for half an hour, then put it into a tin to bake, and wet it with a little treacle and water; if you have a quick oven an hour and a half will bake it.

249. *To make* CHOCOLATE CREAM.

Take four ounces of chocolate, more or less, according as you would have your dish in bigness, grate it and boil it in a pint of cream, then mill it very well with a chocolate stick; take the yolks of two eggs and beat them very well, leaving out the strain, put to them three or four spoonfuls of cream, mix them all together, set it on the fire, and keep stirring it till it thicken, but do not let it boil; you must sweeten it to your taste, and keep stirring it till it be cold, so put it into your glasses or china dishes, which you please.

250. *To make white* LEMON CREAM.

Take a jill of spring water and a pound of fine sugar, set it over a fire till the sugar and water be dissolv'd, then put the juice of four good lemons to your sugar and water, the whites of four eggs well beat, set it on the fire again, and keep it stirring one way till it just simmers and does not boil, strain it thro' a fine cloth, then put it on the fire again, adding to it a spoonful of orange-flower water, stir it till it thickens on a slow fire, then strain into basons or glasses for your use; do not let it boil, if you do it will curdle.

251. *To make* CREAM CURDS.

Take a gallon of water, put to it a quart of new milk, a little salt, a pint of sweet cream and eight eggs, leaving out half the whites and strains, beat them very well, put to them a pint of sour cream, mix them very well together, and when your pan is just at boiling (but is must not boil) put in the sour cream and your eggs, stir it about and keep it from settling to the bottom; let it stand whilst it begins to rise up, then have a little fair water, and as they rise keep putting it in whilst they be well risen, then take them off the fire, and let them stand a little to sadden; have ready a sieve with a clean cloth over it, and take up the curds with a laddle or egg-slicer, whether you have; you must always make them the night before you use them; this quantity will make a large dish if your cream be good; if you think your curds be too thick, mix tho them two or three spoonfuls of good cream, lie them upon a china dish in lumps, so serve them up.

252. *To make* APPLE CREAM.

Take half a dozen large apples, (coslings or any other apples that will be soft) and coddle them; when they are cold take out the pulp; then take the whites of four or five eggs, (leaving out the strains) three quarters of a pound of double-refined sugar beat and sifted, a spoonful or two of rose-water and grate in a little lemon-peel, so beat all together for an hour, whilst it be white, then lay it on a china dish, to serve it up.

253. *To fry* CREAM *to eat hot*.

Take a pint of cream and boil it, three spoonfuls of London flour, mix'd with a little milk, put in three eggs, and beat them very well with the flour, a little salt, a spoonful or two of fine powder sugar, mix them very well; then put your cream to them on the fire and boil it; then beat two eggs more very well, and when you take your pan off the fire stir them in, and pour them into a large pewter dish, about half an inch thick; when it is quite cold cut it out in square bits, and fry it in butter, a light brown; as you fry them set them before the fire to keep hot and crisp, so dish them up with a little white wine, butter and sugar for your sauce, in a china cup, set it in the midst, and grate over some loaf sugar.

254. *To make* RICE *or* ALMOND CREAM.

Take two quarts of cream, boil it with what seasoning you please, then take it from the fire and sweeten it, pick out the seasoning and divide it into two parts, take a quarter of a pound of blanch'd almonds well beat with orange-flower water, set that on the fire, and put to it the yolks of four eggs well beat and strained, keep it stirring all the time it is on the fire, when it rises to boil take it off, stir it a little, then put it into your bason, the other half set on the fire, and thicken it with flour of rice; when you take it off put to it the juice of a lemon, orange-flower water or sack, and stir it till it be cold, then serve it up.

255. *To make* CALF'S FOOT JELLY.

Take four calf's feet and dress them, boil them in six quarts of water over a slow fire, whilst all the bones will come out, and half the water be boiled away, strain it into a stone-bowl, then put to them two or three quarts more water, and let it boil away to one: If you want a large quantity of flummery or jelly at one time; take two calf's feet more, it will make your stock the stronger; you must make your stock the day before you use it, and before you put your stock into the pan take off the fat, and put it into your pan to melt, take the whites of eight or ten eggs, just as you have jelly in quantity, (for the more whites you have makes your jelly the finer) beat your whites to a froth, and put to them five or six lemons, according as they are of goodness, a little white wine or rhenish, mix them well together (but let not your stock be too hot when you put them in) and sweeten it to your taste; keep it stirring all the time whilst it boil; take your bag and dip it in hot water, and wring it well out, then put in your jelly, and keep it shifting whilst it comes clear; throw a lemon-peel or two into your bag as the jelly is coming off, and put in some bits of peel into your glasses.

You may make hartshorn jelly the same way.

256. *To make* ORANGE CREAM.

Take two seville oranges and peel them very thin, put the peel into a pint of fair water, and let it lie for an hour or two; take four eggs, and beat them very well, put to them the juice of three or four oranges, according as they are in goodness, and sweeten them with double refin'd sugar to your taste, mix the water and sugar together, and strain them thro' a fine cloth into your tankard, and set it over the fire as you did the lemon cream, and put it into your glasses for use.

257. *To make yellow* LEMON CREAM.

Take two or three lemons, according as they are in bigness, take off the peel as thin as you can from the white, put it into a pint of clear water, and let it lie three or four hours; take the yolks of three or four eggs, beat them very well, about eight ounces of double refin'd sugar, put it into your water to dissolve, and a spoonful or two of rose-water or orange-flower water, which you can get, mix all together with the juice of two of your lemons, and if your lemons prove not good, put in the juice of three, so strain them through a fine cloth into a silver tankard, and set it over a stove or chafing dish, stirring it all the time, and when it begins to be as thick as cream take it off, but don't let it boil, if you do it will curdle, stir it whilst it be cold and put it into glasses for use.

258. *To make white* LEMON CREAM *another Way.*

Take a pint of spring water, and the whites of six eggs, beat them very well to a froth, put them to your water, adding to it half a pound of double refin'd sugar, a spoonful of orange-flower water, and the juice of three lemons, so mix all together, and strain them through a fine close into your silver tankard, set it over a slow fire in a chafing dish, and keep stirring it all the time; as you see it thickens take it off, it will soon curdle then be yellow, stir it whilst it be cold, and put it in small jelly glasses for use.

259. *To make* SAGOO CUSTARDS.

Take two ounces of sagoo, wash it in a little water, set it on to cree in a pint of milk, and let it cree till it be tender, when it is cold put to it three jills of cream, boil it altogether with a blade or two of mace, or a stick of cinnamon; take six eggs, leave out the strains, beat them very well, mix a little of your cream amongst your eggs, then mix altogether, keep stirring it as you put it in, so set it over a slow fire, and stir it about whilst it be the thickness of a good cream; you must not let it boil; when you take it off the fire put in a tea cupfull of brandy, and sweeten it to your taste, then put it into pots or glasses for use. You may have half the quantity if you please.

260. *To make* ALMOND CUSTARDS.

Boil two quarts of sweet cream with a stick of cinnamon; take eight eggs, leaving out all the whites but two, beat them very well; take six ounces of Jordan almonds, blanch and beat them with a little rose-water, so give them a boil in your cream; put in half a pound of powder sugar, and a little of your cream amongst your eggs, mix altogether, and set them over a slow fire, stir it all the time whilst it be as thick as cream, but don't let it boil; when you take it off put in a little brandy to your taste, so put it into your cups for use.

You may make rice-custard the same way.

261. *To make a* SACK POSSET.

Take a quart of cream, boil it with two or three blades of mace, and grate in a long bisket; take eight eggs, leave out half the whites, beat them very well, and a pint of gooseberry wine, make it hot, so mix it well with your eggs, set it over a slow fire, and stir it about whilst it be as thick as custard; set a dish that is deep over a stove, put in your sack and eggs, when your cream is boiling hot, put it to your sack by degrees, and stir it all the time it stands over your stove, whilst it be thoroughly hot, but don't let it boil; you must make it about half an hour before you want it; set it upon a hot harth, and then it will be as thick as custard; make a little froth of cream, to lay over the posset; when you dish it up sweeten it to your taste; you may make it without bisket if you please, and don't lay on your froth till you serve it up.

262. *To make a* LEMON POSSET.

Take a pint of good thick cream, grate into it the outermost skin of two lemons, and squeeze the juice into a jack of white wine, and sweeten it to your taste; take the whites of two eggs without the strains, beat them to a froth, so whisk them altogether in a stone bowl for half an hour, then put them into glasses for use.

263. *To make whipt* SILLABUBS.

Take two porringers of cream and one of white wine, grate in the skin of a lemon, take the whites of three eggs, sweeten it to your taste, then whip it with a whisk, take off the froth as it rises, and put it into your sillabub-glasses or pots, whether you have, then they are fit for use.

264. *To make* ALMOND BUTTER.

Take a quart of cream, and half a pound of almonds, beat them with the cream, then strain it, and boil it with twelve yolks of eggs and two whites, till it curdle, hang it up in a cloth till morning and then sweeten it; you may rub it through a sieve with the back of a spoon, or strain it through a coarse cloth.

265. *To make* BLACK CAPS.

Take a dozen of middling pippens and cut them in two, take out the cores and black ends, lay them with the flat side downwards, set them in the oven, and when they are about half roasted take them out, wet them over with a little rose water, and grate over them loaf sugar, pretty thick, set them into the oven again, and let them stand till they are black; when you serve them up, put them either into cream or custard, with the black side upwards, and set them at an equal distance.

266. *To make* SAUCE *for tame* DUCKS.

Take the necks and gizzards of your ducks, a scrag of mutton if you have it, and make a little sweet gravy, put to it a few bread-crumbs, a small onion, and a little whole pepper, boil them for half a quarter of an hour, put to them a lump of butter, and if it is not thick enough a little flour, so salt it to your taste.

267. *To make* SAUCE *for a* GREEN-

GOOSE.

Take a little good gravy, a little butter, and a few scalded gooseberries, mix all together, and put it on the disk with your goose.

268. *To make another* SAUCE *for a* GREEN-GOOSE.

Take the juice of sorrel, a little butter, and a few scalded gooseberries, mix them together, and sweeten it to your taste; you must not let it boil after you put in the sorrel, if you do it will take off the green.

You must put this sauce into a bason.

269. *To make* ALMOND FLUMMERY.

Take a pint of stiff jelly made of calf's feet, put to it a jill or better of good cream, and four ounces of almonds, blanch and beat them fine with a little rose-water, then put them to your cream and jelly, let them boil together for half a quarter of an hour, and sweeten it to your taste; strain it through a fine cloth, and keep it stirring till it be quite cold, put it in cups and let it stand all night, loosen it in warm water and turn it out into your dish; so serve it up, and prick it with blanch'd almonds.

270. *To make* CALF'S FOOT FLUMMERY.

Take two calf's feet, when they are dress'd, put two quarts of water to them, boil them over a slow fire till half or better be consumed; when your stock is cold, if it be too stiff, you may put to it as much cream as jelly, boil them together with a blade or two of mace, sweeten it to your taste with loaf sugar, strain it through a fine cloth, stir it whilst it be cold, and turn it out, but first loosen it in warm water, and put it into your dish as you did the other flummery.

271. *To stew* SPINAGE *with* POACHED EGGS.

Take two or three handfuls of young spinage, pick it from the stalks, wash and drain it very clean, put it into a pan with a lump of butter, and a little salt, keep stirring it all the time whilst it be enough, then take it out and squeeze out the water, chop it and stir in a little more butter, lie it in your dish in quarters, and betwixt every quarter a poached egg, and lie one in the middle; fry some sippets of white bread and prick them in your spinage, to serve them up.

This is proper for a side-dish either for noon or night.

272. *To make* RATIFIE DROPS.

Take half a pound of the best jordan almonds, and four ounces of bitter almonds, blanch and set them before the fire to dry, beat them in a marble mortar with a little white of an egg, then put to the half a pound of powder sugar, and beat them altogether to a pretty stiff paste; you may beat your white of egg very well before you put it in, so take it out, roll it with your hand upon a board with a little sugar, then cut them in pieces, and lie them on sheets of tin or on paper, at an equal distance, that they don't touch one another, and set them in a slow oven to bake.

273. *To fry* ARTICHOKE BOTTOMS.

Take artichoke bottoms when they are at the full growth, and boil them as you would do for eating, pull off the leaves, and take out the choke, cut off the stalks as close as you can from the bottom; take two or three eggs, beat them very well, so dip your artichokes in them, and strow over them a little pepper and salt; fry them in butter, some whole and some in halves; serve them up with a little butter in a china cup, set it in the middle of your dish, lie your artichokes round, and serve them up.

They are proper for a side dish either noon or night.

274. *To fricassy* ARTICHOKES.

Take artichokes, and order them the same way as you did for frying, have ready in a stew-pan a few morels and truffles, stewed in brown gravy, so put in your artichokes, and give them a shake altogether in your stew-pan, and serve them up hot, with sippets round them.

275. *To dry* ARTICHOKE BOTTOMS.

Take the largest artichokes you can get, when they are at their full growth, boil them as you would do for eating, pull off the leaves and take out the choke; cut off the stalk as close as you can, lie them on a tin dripping-pan, or an earthen dish, set them in a slow oven, for if your oven be too hot it will brown them; you may dry them before the fire if you have conveniency; when they are dry put them in paper bags, and keep them for use.

276. *To stew* APPLES.

Take a pound of double refin'd sugar, with a pint of water, boil and skim it, and put into it a pound of the largest and clearest pippens, pared and cut in halves; if little, let them be whole; core them and boil them with a continual froth, till they be as tender and clear as you would have them, put in the juice of two lemons, but first take out the apples, a little peel cut like threads, boil down your syrrup as thick as you would have it, then pour it over your apples; when you dish them, stick them with long bits of candid orange, and some with almonds cut in long bits, to serve them up.

You must stew them the day before you use them.

277. *To stew* APPLES *another Way*.

Take kentish pippens or john apples, pare and slice them into fair water, set them on a clear fire, and when they are boiled to mash, let the liquor run through a hair-sieve; boil as many apples thus as will make the quantity of liquor you would have; to a pint of this liquor you must have a pound of double refin'd loaf sugar in great lumps, wet the lumps of sugar with the pippen liquor, and set it over a gentle fire, let it boil, and skim it well: whilst you are making the jelly, you must have your whole pippens boiling at the same time; (they must be the fairest and best pippens you can get) scope out the cores, and pare them neatly, put them into fair water as you do them; you must likewise make a syrrup ready to put them into, the quantity as you think will boil them in a clear; make the syrrup with double refin'd sugar and water. Tie up your whole pippens in a piece of fine cloth or muslin severally, when your sugar and water boils put them in, let them boil very fast, so fast that the syrrup always boils over them; sometimes take them off, and then set them on again, let them boil till they be clear and tender; then take off the muslin they were tied up in, and put them into glasses that will hold but one in a glass; then see if your jelly of apple-johns be boiled to jelly enough, if it be, squeeze in the juice of two lemons, and let it have a boil; then strain it through a jelly bag into the glasses your pippens were in; you must be sure that your pippens be well drained from the syrrup they were boiled in; before you put them into the glasses, you may, if you please, boil little pieces of lemon-peel in water till they be tender, and then boil them in the syrrup your pippens were boiled in; then take them out and lay them upon the pippens before the jelly is put in, and when they are cold paper them up.

278. *To make* PLUMB GRUEL.

Take half a pound of pearl barley, set it on to cree; put to it three quarts of water; when it has boiled a while, shift it into another fresh water, and put to it three or four blades of mace, a little lemon-peel cut in long pieces, so let it boil whilst the barley be very soft; if it be too thick you may add a little more water; take half a pound of currans, wash them well and plump them, and put to them your barley, half a pound of raisins and stone them; let them boil in the gruel whilst they are plump, when they are enough put to them a little white wine, a little juice of lemon, grate in half a nutmeg, and sweeten it to your taste, so serve them up.

279. *To make* RICE GRUEL.

Boil half a pound of rice in two quarts of soft water, as soft as you would have it for rice milk, with some slices of lemon-peel, and a stick of cinnamon; add to it a little white wine and juice of lemon to your taste, put in a little candid orange sliced thin, and sweeten it with fine powder sugar; don't let it boil after you put in your wine and lemon, put it in a china dish, with five or six slices of lemon, so serve it up.

280. *To make* SCOTCH CUSTARD, *to eat hot for Supper*.

Boil a quart of cream with a stick of cinnamon, and a blade of mace; take six eggs, both yolks and whites (leave out the strains) and beat them very well, grate a long bisket into your cream, give it a boil before you put in your eggs, mix a little of your cream amongst your eggs before you put 'em in, so set it over a slow fire, stirring it about whilst it be thick, but don't let it boil; take half a pound of currans, wash them very well, and plump them, then put them to your custard; you must let your custard be as thick as will bear the currans that they don't sink to the bottom; when you are going to dish it up, put in a large glass of sack, stir it very well, and serve it up in a china bason.

281. *To make a Dish of* MULL'D MILK.

Boil a quart of new milk with a stick of cinnamon, then put to it a pint of cream, and let them have one boil together, take eight eggs, (leave out half of the whites and all the strains) beat them very well, put to them a jill of milk, mix all together, and set it over a slow fire, stir it whilst it begins to thicken like custard, sweeten it to your taste, and grate in half a nutmeg; then put it into your dish with a toast of white bread.

This is proper for a supper.

282. *To make* LEATCH.

Take two ounces of isinglass and break it into bits, put it into hot water, then put half a pint of new milk into the pan with the isinglass, set it on the fire to boil, and put into it three or four sticks of good cinnamon, two blades of mace, a nutmeg quartered, and two or three cloves, boil it till the isinglass be dissolved, run it through a hair-sieve into a large pan, then put to it a quart of cream sweetened to your taste with loaf sugar, and boil them a while together; take a quarter of a pound of blanch'd almonds beaten in a rose-water, and strain out all the juice of them into the cream on the fire, and warm it, then take it off and stir it well together; when it has cooled a little take a broad shallow dish and put it into it through a hair-sieve, when it is cold cut it in long pieces, and lay it across whilst you have a pretty large dish; so serve it up.

Sometimes a less quantity of isinglass will do, according to the goodness; Let it be the whitest and clearest you can get.

You must make it the day before you want it for use.

283. *To make* SCOTCH OYSTERS.

Take two pounds of the thick part of a leg of veal, cut it in little bits clear from the skins, and put it in a marble mortar, then shred a pound of beef suet and put to it, and beat them well together till they be as fine as paste; put to it a handful of bread-crumbs and two or three eggs, season it with mace, nutmeg, pepper, and salt, and work it well together; take one part of your forc'd-meat and wrap it in the kell, about the bigness of a pigeon, the rest make into little flat cakes and fry them; the rolls you may either broil in a dripping-pan, or set them in an oven; three is enough in a dish, set them in the middle of the dish and lay the cakes round; then take some strong gravy, shred in a few capers, and two or three mushrooms or oysters if you have any, so thicken it up with a lump of butter, and serve it up hot. Garnish your dish with pickles.

284. *To boil* BROCOLI.

Take brocoli when it is seeded, or at any other time; take off all the low leaves of your stalks and tie them up in bunches as you do asparagus, cut them the same length you peel your stalks; cut them in little pieces, and boil them in salt and water by themselves; you must let your water boil before you put them in; boil the heads in salt and water, and let the water boil before you put in the brocoli; put in a little butter; it takes very little boiling, and if it boil too quick it will take off all the heads; you must drain your brocoli through a sieve as you do asparagus; lie stalks in the middle, and the bunches round it, as you would do asparagus.

This is proper for either a side-dish or a middle-dish.

285. *To boil* SAVOY SPROUTS.

If your savoys be cabbag'd, dress off the out leaves and cut them in quarters; take off a little of the hard ends, and boil them in a large quantity of water with a little salt; when boiled drain them, lie them round your meat, and pour over them a little butter.

Any thing will boil greener in a large

quantity of water than otherwise.

286. *To boil* CABBAGE SPROUTS.

Take your sprouts, cut off the leaf and the hard ends, shred and boil them as you do other greens, not forgetting a little butter.

287. *To fry* PARSNIPS *to look like* TROUT.

Take a middling sort of parsnips, not over thick, boil them as soft as you would do for eating, peel and cut them in two the long way; you must only fry the small ends, not the thick ones; beat three or four eggs, put to them a spoonful of flour, dip in your parsnips, and fry them in butter a light brown have for your sauce a little vinegar and butter; fry some slices to lie round about the dish, and to serve them up.

288. *To make* TANSEY *another Way*.

Take an old penny loaf and cut off the crust, slice it thin, put to it as much hot cream as will wet it, then put to it six eggs well beaten, a little shred lemon-peel, a little nutmeg and salt, and sweeten it to your taste; green it as you did your baked tansey; so tie it up in a cloth and boil it; (it will take an hour and a quarter boiling) when you dish it up stick it with a candid orange, and lie a sevile orange cut in quarters round your dish; serve it up with a little plain butter.

289. *To make* GOOSEBERRY CREAM.

Take a quart of gooseberries, pick, coddle, and bruise them very well in a marble mortar or wooden bowl, and rub them with the back of a spoon through a hair sieve, till you take out all the pulp from the seeds; take a pint of thick cream, mix it well among your pulp grate in some lemon-peel, and sweeten it to your taste; serve it up either in a china dish or an earthen one.

290. *To fry* PARSNIPS *another Way*.

Boil your parsnips, cut them in square long pieces about the length of your finger, dip them in egg and a little flour, and fry them a light brown; when they are fried dish them up, and grate over them a little sugar: You must have for the sauce a little white wine, butter, and sugar in a bason, and set in the middle of your dish.

291. *To make* APRICOCK PUDDING.

Take ten apricocks, pare, stone, and cut them in two, put them into a pan with a quarter of a pound of loaf sugar, boil them pretty quick whilst they look clear, so let them stand whilst they are cold; then take six eggs, (leave out half of the whites) beat them very well, add to them a pint of cream, mix the cream and eggs well together with a spoonful of rose-water, then put in your apricocks, and beat them very well together, with four ounces of clarified butter, then put it into your dish with a thin paste under it; half an hour will bake it.

292. *To make* APRICOCK CUSTARD.

Take a pint of cream, boil it with a stick of cinnamon and six eggs, (leave out four of the whites) when your cream is a little cold, mix your eggs and cream together, with a quarter of a pound of fine sugar, set it over a slow fire, stir it all one way whilst it begin to be thick, then take it off and stir it whilst it be a little cold, and pour it into your dish; take six apricocks, as you did for your pudding, rather a little higher; when they are cold lie them upon your custard at an equal distance; if it be at the time when you have no ripe apricocks, you may lie preserv'd apricocks.

293. *To make* JUMBALLS *another Way*.

Take a pound of meal and dry it, a pound of sugar finely beat, and mix these together; then take the yolks of five or six eggs, half a jill of thick cream, as much as will make it up to a paste, and some coriander seeds, lay them on tins and prick them; bake them in a quick oven; before you set them in the oven wet them with a little rose-water and double refin'd sugar to ice them.

294. *To make* APRICOCK CHIPS *or* PEACHES.

Take a pound of chips to a pound of sugar, let not your apricocks be too ripe, pare them and cut them into large chips; take three quarters of a pound of fine sugar, strow most of it upon the chips, and let them stand till they be dissolv'd, set them on the fire, and boil them till they are tender and clear, strowing the remainder of the sugar on as they boil, skim them clear, and lay them in glasses or pots single, with some syrrup, cover them with double refin'd sugar, set them in a stove, and when they are crisp on one side turn the other on glasses and parch them, then set them into the stove again; when they are pretty dry, pour them on hair-sieves till they are dry enough to put up.

295. *To make* SAGOO GRUEL.

Take four ounces of sagoo and wash it, set it over a slow fire to cree, in two quarts of spring water, let it boil whilst it be thickish and soft, put in a blade or two of mace, and a stick of cinnamon, let it boil in a while, and then put in a little more water; take it off, put to it a pint of claret wine, and a little candid orange; shift them, then put in the juice of a lemon, and sweeten it to your taste; so serve them up.

296. *To make* SPINAGE TOASTS.

Take a handful or two of young spinage and wash it, drain it from the water, put it into a pan with a lump of butter, and a little salt, let it stew whilst it be tender, only turn it in the boiling, then take it up and squeeze out the water, put in another lump of butter and chop it small, put to it a handful of currans plump'd, and a little nutmeg; have three toasts cut from a penny loaf well buttered, then lie on your spinage.

This is proper for a side-dish either for noon or night.

297. *To roast a* BEAST KIDNEY.

Take a beast kidney with a little fat on, and stuff it all around, season it with a little pepper and salt, wrap it in a kell, and put it upon the spit with a little water in the dripping-pan; what drops from your kidney thicken with a lump of butter and flour for your sauce.

To fry your STUFFING.

Take a handful of sweet herbs, a few breadcrumbs, a little beef-suet shred fine, and two eggs, (leave out the whites) mix altogether with a little nutmeg, pepper and salt; stuff your kidney with one part of the stuffing, and fry the other part in little cakes; so serve it up.

298. *To stew* CUCUMBERS.

Take middling cucumbers and cut them in slices, but not too thin, strow over them a little salt to bring out the water, put them into a stew-pan or sauce-pan, with a little gravy, some whole pepper, a lump of butter, and a spoonful or two of vinegar to your taste; let them boil all together; thicken them with flour, and serve them up with sippets.

299. *To make an* OATMEAL PUDDING.

Take three or four large spoonfuls of oatmeal done through a hair-sieve, and a pint of milk, put it into a pan and let it boil a little whilst it be thick, add to it half a pound of butter, a spoonful of rose-water, a little lemon-peel shred, a little nutmeg, or beaten cinnamon, and a little salt; take six eggs, (leave out two of the whites) and put to them a quarter of a pound of sugar or better, beat them very well, so mix them all together; put it into your dish with a paste round your dish edge; have a little rose-water, butter and sugar for sauce.

300. *To make a* CALF'S HEAD PIE *another Way*.

Half boil your calf's head, when it is cold cut it in slices, rather thicker than you would do for hashing, season it with a little mace, nutmeg, pepper and salt, lie part of your meat in the bottom of your pie, a layer of one and a layer of another; then put in half a pound of butter and a little gravy; when your pie comes from the oven, have ready the yolks of six or eight eggs boiled hard, and lie them round your pie; put in a little melted butter, and a spoonful or two of white wine, and give them a shake together before you lie in your eggs; your pie must be a standing pie baked upon a dish, with a puff-paste round the edge of the dish, but leave no paste in the bottom of your pie; when it is baked serve it up without a lid.

This is proper for either top or bottom dish.

301. *To make* ELDER WINE.

Take twenty pounds of malaga raisins, pick and chop them, then put them into a tub with twenty quarts of water, let the water be boiled and stand till it be cold again before you put in your raisins, let them remain together ten days, stirring it twice a day, then strain the liquor very well from the raisins, through a canvas strainer or hair-sieve; add to it six quarts of elder juice, five pounds of loaf sugar, and a little juice of sloes to make it acid, just as you please; put it into a vessel, and let it stand in a pretty warm place three months, then bottle it; the vessel must not be stopp'd up till it has done working; if your raisins be very good you may leave out the sugar.

302. *To make* GOOSEBERRY WINE *of ripe* GOOSEBERRIES.

Pick, clean and beat your gooseberries in a marble mortar or wooden bowl, measure them in quarts up-heap'd, add two quarts of spring water, and let them stand all night or twelve hours, then rub or press out the husks very well, strain them through a wide strainer, and to every gallon put three pounds of sugar, and a jill of brandy, then put all into a sweet vessel, not very full, and keep it very close for four months, then decant it off till it comes clear, pour out the grounds, and wash the vessel clean with a little of the wine; add to every gallon a pound more sugar, let it stand a month in a vessel again, drop the grounds thro' a flannel bag, and put it to the other in the vessel; the tap hole must not be over near the bottom of the cask, for fear of letting out the grounds.

The same receipt will serve for curran wine the same way; let them be red currans.

303. *To make* BALM WINE.

Take a peck of balm leaves, put them in a tub or large pot, heat four gallons of water scalding hot, ready to boil, then pour it upon the leaves, so let it stand all night, then strain them thro' a hair-sieve; put to every gallon of water two pounds of fine sugar, and stir it very well; take the whites of four or five eggs, beat them very well, put them into a pan, and whisk it very well before it be over hot, when the skim begins to rise take it off, and keep it skimming all the while it is boiling, let it boil three quarters of an hour, then put it into the tub, when it is cold put a little new yeast upon it, and beat it in every two hours, that it may head the better, so work it for two days, then put it into a sweet rundlet, bung it up close, and when it is fine bottle it.

304. *To make* RAISIN WINE.

Take ten gallons of water, and fifty pounds of malaga raisins, pick out the large stalks and boil them in your water, when your water is boiled, put it into a tub; take the raisins and chop them very small, when your water is blood warm, put in your raisins, and rub them very well with your hand; when you put them into the water, let them work for ten days, stirring them twice a day, then strain out the raisins in a hair-sieve, and put them into a clean harden bag, and squeeze it in the press to take out the liquor, so put it into your barrel; don't let it be over full, bung it up close, and let it stand whilst it is fine; when you tap your wine you must not tap it too near the bottom, for fear of the grounds; when it is drawn off, take the grounds out of the barrel, and wash it out with a little of your wine, then put your wine into the barrel again, draw your grounds thro' a flannel bag, and put them into the barrel to the rest; add to it two pounds of loaf sugar, then bung it up, and let it stand a week or ten days; if it be very sweet to your taste, let it stand some time longer, and bottle it.

305. *To make* BIRCH WINE.

Take your birch water and boil it, clear it with whites of eggs; to every gallon of water take two pounds and a half of fine sugar, boil it three quarters of an hour, and when it is almost cold, put in a little yeast, work it two or three days, then put it into the barrel, and to every five gallons put in a quart of brandy, and half a pound of ston'd raisins; before you put up your wine burn a brimstone match in the barrel.

306. *To make* WHITE CURRAN WINE.

Take the largest white currans you can get, strip and break them in your hand, whilst you break all the berries; to every quart of pulp take a quart of water, let the water be boiled and cold again, mix them well together, let them stand all night in your tub, then strain them thro' a hair-sieve, and to every gallon put two pounds and a half of sixpenny sugar; when your sugar is dissolved, put it into your barrel, dissolve a little isinglass, whisk it with whites of eggs, and put it in; to every four gallons put in a quart of mountain wine, so bung up your barrel; when it is fine draw it off, and take off the grounds, (but don't tap the barrel over low at the bottom) wash out the barrel with a little of your wine, and drop the grounds thro' a bag, then put it to the rest of your wine, and put it all into your barrel again, to every gallon add half a pound more sugar, and let it stand another week or two; if it be too sweet let it stand a little longer, then bottle it, and it will keep two or three years.

307. *To make* ORANGE ALE.

Take forty seville oranges, pare and cut them in slices, the best coloured seville you can get, put them all with the juice and seeds into half a hogshead of ale; when it is tunned up and working, put in the oranges, and at the same time a pound and a half of raisins of the sun stoned; when it has done working close up the bung, and it will be ready to drink in a month.

308. *To make* ORANGE BRANDY.

Take a quart of brandy, the peels of eight oranges thin pared, keep them in the brandy forty-eight hours in a close pitcher, then take three pints of water, put into it three quarters of a pound of loaf sugar, boil it till half be consumed, and let it stand till cold, then mix it with the brandy.

309. *To make* ORANGE WINE.

Take six gallons of water and fifteen pounds of powder sugar, the whites of six eggs well beaten, boil them three quarters of an hour, and skim them while any skim will rise; when it is cold enough for working, put to it six ounces of the syrrup of citron or lemons, and six spoonfuls of yeast, beat the syrrup and yeast well together, and put in the peel and juice of fifty oranges, work it two days and a night, then tun it up into a barrel, so bottle it at three or four months old.

310. *To make* COWSLIP WINE.

Take ten gallons of water, when it is almost at boiling, add to it twenty one pounds of fine powder sugar, let it boil half an hour, and skim it very clean; when it is boiled put it in a tub, let it stand till you think it cold to set on the yeast; take a poringer of new yeast off the fat, and put to it a few cowslips; when you put on the yeast, put in a few every time it is stirred, till all the cowslips be in, which must be six pecks, and let it work three or four days; add to it six lemons, cut off the peel, and the insides put into your barrel, then add to it a pint of brandy; when you think it has done working, close up your vessel, let it stand a month, and then bottle it; you may let your cowslips lie a week or ten days to dry before you make your wine, for it makes it much finer; you may put in a pint of white wine that is good, instead of the brandy.

311. *To make* ORANGE WINE *another Way*.

Take six gallons of water, and fifteen pounds of sugar, put your sugar into the water on the fire, the whites of six eggs, well beaten, and whisk them into the water, when it is cold skim it very well whilst any skim rises, and let it boil for half an hour; take fifty oranges, pare them very thin, put them into your tub, pour the water boiling hot upon your oranges, and when it is bloodwarm put on the yeast, then put in your juice, let it work two days, and so tun it into your barrel; at six weeks or two months old bottle it; you may put to it in the barrel a quart of brandy.

312. *To make* BIRCH WINE *another Way*.

To a gallon of birch water put two pounds of loaf or very fine lump sugar, when you put it into the pan whisk the whites of four eggs; (four whites will serve for four gallons) whisk them very well together before it be boiled, when it is cold put on a little yeast, let it work a night and a day in the tub, before you put it into your barrel put in a brimstone match burning; take two pounds of isinglass cut in little bits, put to it a little of your wine, let it stand within the air of the fire all night; takes the whites of two eggs, beat it with your isinglass, put them into your barrel and stir them about with a stick; this quantity will do for four gallons; to four gallons you must have two pounds of raisins shred, put them into your barrel, close it up, but not too close at the first, when it is fine, bottle it.

313. *To make* APRICOCK WINE.

Take twelve pounds of apricocks when full ripe, stone and pare them, put the paring into three gallons of water, with six pounds of powder sugar, boil them together half an hour, skim them well, and when it is blood-warm put it on the fruit; it must be well bruised, cover it close, and let it stand three days; skim it every day as the skim rises, and put it thro' a hair sieve, adding a pound of loaf sugar; when you put it into the vessel close it up, and when it is fine bottle it.

314. *To make* ORANGE SHRUB.

Take seville oranges when they are full ripe, to three dozen of oranges put half a dozen of large lemons, pare them very thin, the thinner the better, squeeze the lemons and oranges together, strain the juice thro' a hair sieve, to a quart of the juice put a pound and a quarter of loaf sugar; about three dozen of oranges (if they be good) will make a quart of juice, to every quart of juice, put a gallon of brandy, put it into a little barrel with an open bung with all the chippings of your oranges, and bung it up close; when it is fine bottle it.

This is a pleasant dram, and ready for punch all the year.

315. *To make* STRONG MEAD.

Take twelve gallons of water, eight pounds of sugar, two quarts of honey, and a few cloves, when your pan boils take the whites of eight or ten eggs, beat them very well, put them into your water before it be hot, and whisk them very well together; do not let it boil but skim it as it rises till it has done rising, then put it into your tub; when it is about blood warm put to it three spoonfuls of new yeast; take eight or nine lemons, pare them and squeeze out the juice, put them both together into your tub, and let them work two or three days, then put it into your barrel, but it must not be too full; take two or three pennyworth of isinglass, cut as small as you can, beat it in a mortar about a quarter of an hour, it will not make it small; but that it may dissolve sooner, draw out a little of the mead into a quart mug, and let it stand within the air of the fire all night; take the whites of three eggs, beat them very well, mix them with your isinglas, whisk them together, and put them into your barrel, bung it up, and when it is fine bottle it.

You may order isinglass this way to put into any sort of made wine.

316. *To make* MEAD *another Way*.

Take a quart of honey, three quarts of water, put your honey into the water, when it is dissolved, take the whites of four or five eggs, whisk and beat them very well together and put them into your pan; boil it while the skim rises, and skim it very clean; put it into your tub, when it is warm put in two or three spoonfuls of light yeast, according to the quantity of your mead, and let it work two nights and a day. To every gallon put in a large lemon, pare and strain it, put the juice and peel into your tub, and when it is wrought put it into your barrel; let it work for three or four days, stir twice a day with a thible, so bung it up, and let it stand two or three months, according to the hotness of the weather.

You must try your mead two or three times in the above time, and if you find the sweetness going off, you must take it sooner.

317. *To make* CYDER.

Draw off the cyder when it hath been a fortnight in the barrel, put it into the same barrel again when you have cleaned it from the grounds, and if your apples were sharp, and that you find your cyder hard, put into every gallon of cyder a pound and half of sixpenny or five-penny sugar; to twelve gallons of this take half an ounce of isinglass, and put to it a quart of cyder; when your isinglass is dissolved, put to it three whites of eggs, whisk them altogether, and put them into your barrel; keep it close for two months and then bottle it.

318. *To make* COWSLIP WINE.

Take two pecks of peeps, and four gallons of water, put to every gallon of water two pounds and a quarter of sugar, boil the water and sugar together a quarter of an hour, then put it into a tub to cool, put in the skins of four lemons, when it is cold bruise your peeps, and put into your liquor, add to it a jill of yeast, and the juice of four lemons, let them be in the tub a night and a day, then put it into your barrel, and keep it four days stirring, then clay it up close for three weeks and bottle it. Put a lump of sugar in every bottle.

319. *To make* RED CURRAN WINE.

Let your currans be the best and ripest you can get, pick and bruise them; to every gallon of juice add five pints of water, put it to your berries in a stand for two nights and a day, then strain your liquor through a hair sieve; to every gallon of liquor put two pounds of sugar, stir it till it be well dissolved, put it into a rundlet, and let it stand four days, then draw it off clean, put in a pound and a half of sugar, stirring it well, wash out the rundlet with some of the liquor, so tun it up close; if you put two or three quarts of rasps bruised among your berries, it makes it taste the better.

You may make white curran wine the same way, only leave out the rasps.

320. *To make* CHERRY WINE.

Take eight pounds of cherries and stone them, four quarts of water, and two pounds of sugar, skim and boil the water and sugar, then put in the cherries, let them have one boil, put them into an earthen pot till the next day, and set them to drain thro' a sieve, then put your wine into a spigot pot, clay it up close, and look at it every two or three days after; if it does not work, throw into it a handful of fresh cherries, so let it stand six or eight days, then if it be clear, bottle it up.

321. *To make* CHERRY WINE *another Way*.

Take the ripest and largest kentish cherries you can get, bruise them very well, stones and stalks altogether, put them into a tub, having a tap to it, let them stand fourteen days, then pull out the tap, let the juice run from them and put it into a barrel, let it work three or four days, then stop it up close three or four weeks and bottle it off.

The wine will keep many years and be exceeding rich.

322. *To make* LEMON DROPS.

Take a pound of loaf sugar, beat and sift it very fine, grate the rind of a lemon and put into your sugar; take the whites of three eggs and wisk them to a froth, squeeze in some lemon to your taste, beat them for half an hour, and drop them on white paper; be sure you let the paper be very dry, and sift a little fine sugar on the paper before you drop them. If you would have them yellow, take a pennyworth of gumbouge, steep it in some rose-water, mix to it some whites of eggs and a little sugar, so drop them, and bake them in a slow oven.

323. *To make* Gooseberry Wine *another Way*.

Take twelve quarts of good ripe gooseberries, stamp them, and put to them twelve quarts of water, let them stand three days, stir them twice every day, strain them, and put to your liquor fourteen pounds of sugar; when it is dissolved strain it through a flannel bag, and put it into a barrel, with half an ounce of isinglass; you must cut the isinglass in pieces, and beat it whilst it be soft, put to it a pint of your wine, and let it stand within the air of the fire; take the whites of four eggs and beat them very well to a froth, put in the isinglass, and whisk the wine and it together; put them into the barrel, clay it close, and let it stand whilst fine, then bottle it for use.

324. *To make* Red Curran Wine *another Way*.

Take five quarts of red currans, full ripe, bruise them, and take from them all the stalks, to every five quarts of fruit put a gallon of water; when you have your quantity, strain them thro' a hair-sieve, and to every gallon of liquor put two pounds and three quarters of sugar; when your sugar is dissolved tun it into your cask, and let it stand three weeks, then draw it off, and put to every gallon a quarter of a pound of sugar; wash your barrel with cold water, tun it up, and let it stand about a week; to every ten gallons put an ounce of isinglass, dissolve it in some of the wine, when it is dissolved put to it a quart of your wine, and beat them with a whisk, then put it into the cask, and stop it up close; when it is fine bottle it.

If you would have it taste of rasps,

put to every gallon of wine a quart of rasps; if there be any grounds in the bottom of the cask, when you draw off your wine, drop them thro' a flannel bag, and then put it into your cask.

325. *To make* MULBERRY WINE.

Gather your mulberries when they are full ripe, beat them in a marble mortar, and to every quart of berries put a quart of water; when you put 'em into the tub rub them very well with your hands, and let them stand all night, then strain 'em thro' a sieve; to every gallon of water put three pounds of sugar, and when the sugar is dissolved put it into your barrel; take two pennyworth of isinglass and clip it in pieces, put to it a little wine, and let it stand all night within the air of the fire; take the whites of two or three eggs, beat them very well, then put them to the isinglass, mix them well together, and put them into your barrel, stirring it about when it is put in; you must not let it be over full, nor bung it close up at first; set it in a cool place and bottle it when fine.

326. *To make* BLACKBERRY WINE.

Take blackberries when they are full ripe, and squeeze them the same way as you did the mulberries. If you add a few mulberries, it will make your wine have a much better taste.

327. *To make* SYRRUP OF MULBERRIES.

Take mulberries when they are full ripe, break them very well with your hand, and drop them through a flannel bag; to every pound of juice take a pound of loaf sugar; beat it small, put to it your juice, so boil and skim it very well; you must skim it all the time it is boiling; when the skim has done rising it is enough; when it is cold bottle it and keep it for use.

You may make rasberry syrrup the same way.

328. *To make* RASBERRY BRANDY.

Take a gallon of the best brandy you can get, and gather your rasberries when they are full ripe, and put them whole into your brandy; to every gallon of brandy take three quarts of rasps, let them stand close covered for a month, then clear it from rasps, and put to it a pound of loaf sugar; when your sugar is dissolved and a little settled, boil it and keep it for use.

329. *To make Black* CHERRY BRANDY.

Take a gallon of the best brandy, and eight pounds of black cherries, stone and put 'em into your brandy in an earthen pot; bruise the stones in a mortar, then put them into your brandy, and cover them up close, let them steep for a month or six weeks, so drain it and keep it for use.

You may distil the ingredients if you please.

330. *To make* RATIFIE BRANDY.

Take a quart of the best brandy, and about a jill of apricock kernels, blanch and bruise them in a mortar, with a spoonful or two of brandy, so put them into a large bottle with your brandy; put to it four ounces of loaf sugar, let it stand till you think it has got the taste of the kernels, then pour it out and put in a little more brandy if you please.

331. *To make* COWSLIP SYRRUP.

Take a quartern of fresh pick'd cowslips, put to 'em a quart of boiling water, let 'em stand all night, and the next morning drain it from the cowslips; to every pint of water put a pound of fine powder sugar, and boil it over a slow fire; skim it all the time in the boiling whilst the skim has done rising; then take it off, and when it is cold put it into a bottle, and keep it for use.

332. *To make* LEMON BRANDY.

Take a gallon of brandy, chip twenty-five lemons, (let them steep twenty-four hours) the juice of sixteen lemons, a quarter of a pound of almonds blanched and beat, drop it thro' a jelly bag twice, and when it is fine bottle it; sweeten it to your taste with double refined sugar before you put it into your jelly bag. You must make it with the best brandy you can get.

333. *To make* CORDIAL WATER *of* COWSLIPS.

Take two quarts of cowslip peeps, a slip of balm, two sprigs of rosemary, a stick of cinnamon, half an orange peel, half a lemon peel, a pint of brandy, and a pint of ale; lay all these to steep twelve hours, then distil them on a cold still.

334. *To make* MILK PUNCH.

Take two quarts of old milk, a quart of good brandy, the juice of six lemons or oranges, whether you please, and about six ounces of loaf sugar, mix them altogether and drop them thro' a jelly bag; take off the peel of two of the lemons or oranges, and put it into your bag, when it is run off bottle it; 'twill keep as long as you please.

335. *To make* MILK PUNCH *another Way.*

Take three jills of water, a jill of old milk, and a jill of brandy, sweeten it to your taste; you must not put any acid into this for it will make it curdle.

This is a cooling punch to drink in a morning.

336. *To make* PUNCH *another Way.*

Take five pints of boiling water and one quart of brandy, add to it the juice of four lemons or oranges, and about six ounces of loaf sugar; when you have mixed it together strain it thro' a hair sieve or cloth, and put into your bowl the peel of a lemon or orange.

337. *To make* ACID *for* PUNCH.

Take gooseberries at their full growth, pick and beat them in a marble mortar, and squeeze them in a harden bag thro' a press, when you have done run it thro' a flannel bag, and then bottle it in small bottles; put a little oil on every bottle, so keep it for use.

338. *To bottle* GOOSEBERRIES.

Gather your gooseberries when they are young, pick and bottle them, put in the cork loose, set them in a pan of water, with a little hay in the bottom, put them into the pan when the water is cold, let it stand on a slow fire, and mind when they are coddled; don't let the pan boil, if you do it will break the bottles: when they are cold fasten the cork, and put on a little rosin, so keep them for use.

339. *To bottle* DAMSINS.

Take your damsins before they are full ripe, and gather them when the dew is off, pick of the stalks, and put them into dry bottles; don't fill your bottles over full, and cork them as close as you would do for ale, keep them in a cellar, and cover them over with sand.

340. *To preserve Orange Chips to put in glasses.*

Take a seville orange with a clear skin, pare it very thin from the white, then take a pair of scissars and clip it very thin, and boil it in water, shifting it two or three times in the boiling to take out the bitter; then take half a pound of double refined sugar, boil it and skim it, then put in your orange, so let it boil over a slow fire whilst your syrrup be thick, and your orange look clear, then put it into glasses, and cover it with papers dipt in brandy; if you have a quantity of peel you must have the larger quantity of sugar.

341. *To preserve* ORANGES *or* LEMONS.

Take seville oranges, the largest and roughest you can get, clear of spots, chip them very fine, and put them into water for two days, shifting them twice or three times a day, then boil them whilst they are soft: take and cut them into quarters, and take out all the pippens with a penknife, so weigh them, and to every pound of orange, take a pound and half of loaf sugar; put your sugar into a pan, and to every pound of sugar a pint of water, set it over the fire to melt, and when it boils skim it very well, then put in your oranges; if you would have any of them whole, make a little hole at the top, and take out the meat with a tea spoon, set your oranges over a slow fire to boil, and keep them skimming all the while; keep your oranges as much as you can with the skin downwards; you may cover them with a delf-plate, to bear them down in the boiling; let them boil for three quarters of an hour, then put them into a pot or bason, and let them stand two days covered, then boil them again whilst they look clear, and the syrrup be thick, so put them into a pot, and lie close over them a paper dip'd in brandy, and tie a double paper at the top, set them in a cool place, and keep them for use. If you would have your oranges that are whole to look pale and clear, to put in glasses, you must make a syrup of pippen jelly; then take ten or a dozen pippens, as they are of bigness, pare and slice them, and boil them in as much water as will cover them till they be thoroughly tender, so strain your water from the pippens through a hair sieve, then strain it through a flannel bag; and to every pint of jelly take a pound of double refined sugar, set it over a fire to boil, and skim it, let it boil whilst it be thick, then put it into a pot and cover it, but they will keep best if they be put every one in different pots.

342. *To make* JELLY *of* CURRANS.

Take a quartern of the largest and best currans you can get, strip them from the stalks, and put them in a pot, stop them close up, and boil them in a pot of water over the fire, till they be thoroughly coddled and begin to look pale, then put them in a clear hair sieve to drain, and run the liquor thro' a flannel bag, to every pint of your liquor put in a pound of your double refin'd sugar; you must beat the sugar fine, and put it in by degrees, set it over the fire, and boil it whilst any skim will rise, then put it into glasses for ale; the next day clip a paper round, and dip it in brandy to lie on your jelly; if you would have your jelly a light red, put in half of white currans, and in my opinion it looks much better.

343. *To preserve* APRICOCKS.

Take apricocks before they be full ripe, stone and pare 'em; then weigh 'em, and to every pound of apricocks take a pound of double refined sugar, beat it very small, lie one part of your sugar under the apricocks, and the other part at the top, let them stand all night, the next day put them in a stew-pan or brass pan; don't do over many at once in your pan, for fear of breaking, let them boil over a slow fire, skim them very well, and turn them two or three times in the boiling; you must but about half do 'em at the first, and let them stand whilst they be cool, then let them boil whilst your apricocks look clear, and the syrrup thick, put them into your pots or glasses, when they are cold cover them with a paper dipt in brandy, then tie another paper close over your pot to keep out the air.

344. *To make* MARMALADE *of* APRICOCKS.

Take what quantity of apricocks you shall think proper, stone them and put them immediately into a skellet of boiling water, keep them under water on the fire till they be soft, then take them out of the water and wipe them with a cloth, weigh your sugar with your apricocks, weight for weight, then dissolve your sugar in water, and boil it to a candy height, then put in your apricocks, being a little bruised, let them boil but a quarter of a hour, then glass them up.

345. *To know when your* SUGAR *is at* CANDY HEIGHT.

Take some sugar and clarify it till it comes to a candy-height, and keep it still boiling 'till it becomes thick, then stir it with a stick from you, and when it is at candy-height it will fly from your stick like flakes of snow, or feathers flying in the air, and till it comes to that height it will not fly, then you may use it as you please.

346. *To make* Marmalade *of* Quinces *white.*

Take your quinces and coddle them as you do apples, when they are soft pare them and cut them in pieces, as if you would cut them for apple pies, then put your cores, parings, and the waste of your quinces in some water, and boil them fast for fear of turning red until it be a strong jelly; when you see the jelly pretty strong strain it, and be sure you boil them uncovered; add as much sugar as the weight of your quinces into your jelly, till it be boiled to a height, then put in your coddled quinces, and boil them uncovered till they be enough, and set them near the fire to harden.

347. *To make* Quiddeny *of* Red Curranberries.

Put your berries into a pot, with a spoonful or two of water, cover it close, and boil 'em in some water, when you think they are enough strain them, and put to every pint of juice a pound of loaf sugar, boil it up jelly height, and put them into glasses for use.

348. *To preserve* GOOSEBERRIES.

To a pound of ston'd gooseberries put a pound and a quarter of fine sugar, wet the sugar with the gooseberry jelly; take a quart of gooseberries, and two or three spoonfuls of water, boil them very quick, let your sugar be melted, and then put in your gooseberries; boil them till clear, which will be very quickly.

349. *To make little* ALMOND CAKES.

Take a pound of sugar and eight eggs, beat them well an hour, then put them into a pound of flour, beat them together, blanch a quarter of a pound of almonds, and beat them with rose-water to keep 'em from oiling, mix all together, butter your tins, and bake them half an hour.

Half an hour is rather too long for them to stand in the oven.

350. *To preserve* RED GOOSEBERRIES.

Take a pound of sixpenny sugar, and a little juice of currans, put to it a pound and a half of Gooseberries, and let them boil quick a quarter of an hour; but if they be for jam they must boil better than half an hour.

They are very proper for tarts, or to eat as sweet-meats.

351. *To bottle* BERRIES *another Way*.

Gather your berries when they are full grown, pick and bottle them, tie a paper over them, prick it with a pin, and set it in the oven; after you have drawn, and when they are coddled, take them out and when they are cold cork them up; rosin the cork over, and keep them for use.

352. *To keep* BARBERRIES *for* TARTS *all the Year*.

Take barberries when they are full ripe, and pick 'em from the stalk, put them into dry bottles, cork 'em up very close and keep 'em for use.

You may do cranberries the same way.

353. *To preserve* BARBERRIES *for* TARTS.

Take barberries when full ripe, strip them, take their weight in sugar, and as much water as will wet your sugar, give it a boil and skim it; then put in your berries, let them boil whilst they look clear and your syrrup thick, so put them into a pot, and when they are cold cover them up with a paper dip'd in brandy.

354. *To preserve* DAMSINS.

Take damsins before they are full ripe, and pick them, take their weight in sugar, and as much water as will wet your sugar, give it a boil and skim it, then put in your damsins, let them have one scald, and set them by whilst cold, then scald them again, and continue scalding them twice a day whilst your syrrup looks thick, and the damsins clear; you must never let them boil; do 'em in a brass pan, and do not take them out in the doing; when they are enough put them into a pot, and cover them up with a paper dip'd in brandy.

355. *How to keep* DAMSINS *for* TARTS.

Take damsins before they are full ripe, to every quart of damsins put a pound of powder sugar, put them into a pretty broad pot, a layer of sugar and a layer of damsins, tie them close up, set them in a slow oven, and let them have a heat every day whilst the syrrup be thick, and the damsins enough; render a little sheep suet and pour over them, to keep them for use.

356. *To keep* DAMSINS *another Way*.

Take damsins before they be quite ripe, pick off the stalks, and put them into dry bottles; cork them as you would do ale, and keep them in a cool place for use.

357. *To make* MANGO *of* CODLINS.

Take codlins when they are at their full growth, and of the greenest sort, take a little out of the end with the stalk, and then take out the core; lie them in a strong salt and water, let them lie ten days or more, and fill them with the same ingredients as you do other mango, only scald them oftner.

358. *To pickle* CURRANBERRIES.

Take currans either red or white before they are thoroughly ripe; you must not take them from the stalk, make a pickle of salt and water and a little vinegar, so keep them for use.

They are proper for garnishing.

359. *To make* Barberries *instead of preserving*.

Take barberries and lie them in a pot, a layer of barberries and a layer of sugar, pick the seeds out before for garnishing sweet meats, if for sauces put some vinegar to them.

360. *To keep* Asparagus *or* Green Pease *a Year*.

Take green pease, green them as you do cucumbers, and scald them as you do other pickles made of salt and water; let it be always new pickle, and when you would use them boil them in fresh water.

361. *To make white Paste of* PIPPENS.

Take some pippens, pare and cut them in halves, and take out the cores, then boil 'em very tender in fair water, and strain them thro' a sieve, then clarify two pounds of sugar with two whites of eggs, and boil it to a candy height, put two pounds and a half of the pulp of your pippens into it, let it stand over a slow fire drying, keeping it stirring till it comes clear from the bottom of your pan, them lie them upon plates or boards to dry.

362. *To make green Paste of* PIPPENS.

Take green pippens, put them into a pot and cover them, let them stand infusing over a slow fire five or six hours, to draw the redness or sappiness from them and then strain them thro' a hair sieve; take two pounds of sugar, boil it to a candy height, put to it two pounds of the pulp of your pippens, keep it stirring over the fire till it comes clean from the bottom of your pan, then lay it on plates or boards, and set it in an oven or stove to dry.

363. *To make red Paste of* PIPPENS.

Take two pounds of sugar, clarify it, then take rosset and temper it very well with fair water, put it into your syrrup, let it boil till your syrrup is pretty red colour'd with it, then drain your syrrup thro' a fine cloth, and boil it till it be at candy-height, then put to it two pounds and a half of the pulp of pippens, keeping it stirring over the fire till it comes clean from the bottom of the pan, then lie it on plates or boards, so dry them.

364. *To preserve* FRUIT *green*.

Take your fruit when they are green, and some fair water, set it on the fire, and when it is hot put in the apples, cover them close, but they must not boil, so let them stand till thye be soft, and there will be a thin skin on them, peel it off, and set them to cool, then put them in again, let them boil till they be very green, and keep them whole as you can; when you think them ready to take up, make your syrrup for them; take their weight in sugar, and when your syrrup is ready put the apples into it, and boil them very well in it; they will keep all the year near some fire.

You may do green plumbs or other fruit.

365. *To make* ORANGE MARMALADE.

Take three or four seville oranges, grate them, take out the meat, and boil the rinds whilst they are tender; shift them three or four times in the boiling to take out the bitter, and beat them very fine in a marble mortar; to the weight of your pulp take a pound of loaf sugar, and to a pound of sugar you may add a pint of water, boil and skim it before you put in your oranges, let it boil half an hour very quick, then put in your meat, and to a pint take a pound and a half of sugar, let it boil quick half an hour, stir it all the time, and when it is boiled to a jelly, put it into pots or glasses; cover it with a paper dipp'd in brandy.

366. *To make* QUINCES WHITE *another Way.*

Coddle your quinces, cut them in small pieces, and to a pound of quinces take three quarters of a pound of sugar, boil it to a candy height, having ready a quarter of a pint of quince liquor boil'd and skim'd, put the quinces and liquor to your sugar, boil them till it looks clear, which will be very quickly, then close your quince, and when cold cover it with jelly of pippens to keep the colour.

367. *To make* GOOSEBERRY VINEGAR.

To every gallon of water take six pounds of ripe gooseberries, bruise them, and pour the water boiling hot upon your berries, cover it close, and set it in a warm place to foment, till all the berries come to the top, then draw it off, and to every gallon of liquor put a pound and a half of sugar, then tun it into a cask, set it in a warm place, and in six months it will be fit for use.

368. *To make* Gooseberry Wine *another Way.*

Take three pounds of ripe gooseberries to a quart of water, and a pound of sugar, stamp your berries and throw them into your water as you stamp them, it will make them strain the better; when it is strained put in your sugar, beat it well with a dish for half an hour, then strain it thro' a finer strainer than before into your vessel, leaving it some room to work, and when it is clear bottle it; your berries must be clean pick'd before your use them, and let them be at their full growth when you use them, rather changing colour.

369. *To make* Jam of Cherries.

Take ten pounds of cherries, stone and boil them till the juice be wasted, then add to it three pounds of sugar, and give it three or four good boils, then put it into your pots.

370. *To preserve* Cherries.

To a pound of cherries take a pound of sugar finely sifted, with which strow the bottom of your pan, having stoned the cherries, lay a layer of cherries and a layer of sugar, strowing the sugar very well over all, boil them over a quick fire a good while, keeping them clean skim'd till they look clear, and the syrrup is thick and both of one colour; when you think them half done, take them off the fire for an hour, after which set them on again, and to every pound of fruit put in a quarter of a pint of the juice of cherries and red currans, so boil them till enough, and the syrrup is jellied, then put them in a pot, and keep them close from the air.

371. *To preserve* CHERRIES *for drying.*

Take two pounds of cherries and stone them, put to them a pound of sugar, and as much water as will wet the sugar, then set them on the fire, let them boil till they look clear, then take them off the fire, and let them stand a while in the syrrup, and then take them up and lay them on papers to dry.

372. *To preserve* FRUIT *green all the Year.*

Gather your fruit when they are three parts ripe, on a very dry day, when the sun shines on them, then take earthen pots and put them in, cover the pots with cork, or bung them that no air can get into them, dig a place in the earth a yard deep, set the pots therein and cover them with the earth very close, and keep them for use.

When you take any out, cover them up again, as at the first.

373. *How to keep* KIDNEY BEANS *all Winter.*

Take kidney beans when they are young, leave on both the ends, lay a layer of salt at the bottom of your pot, and then a layer of beans, and so on till your pot be full, cover them close at the top that they get no air, and set them in a cool place; before you boil them lay them in water all night, let your water boil when you put them in, (without salt) and put into it a lump of butter about the bigness of a walnut.

374. *To candy* ANGELICA.

Take angelica when it is young and tender take off all the leaves from the stalks, boil it in the pan with some of the leaves under, and some at the top, till it be so tender that you can peel off all the skin, then put it into some water again, cover it over with some of the leaves, let it simmer over a slow fire till it be green, when it is green drain the water from it, and then weigh it; to a pound of angelica take a pound of loaf sugar, put a pint of water to every pound of sugar, boil and skim it, and then put in your angelica; it will take a great deal of boiling in the sugar, the longer you boil it and the greener it will be, boil it whilst your sugar be candy height by the side of your pan; if you would have it nice and white, you must have a pound of sugar boiled candy height in a copperdish or stew pan, set it over a chafing dish, and put it into your angelica, let it have a boil, and it will candy as you take it out.

375. *To dry* PEARS.

Take half a peck of good baking pears, (or as many as you please) pare and put them in a pot, and to a peck of pears put in two pounds of sugar; you must put in no water but lie the parings on the top of your pears, tie them up close, and set them in a brown bread oven; when they are baked lay them in a dripping pan, and flat them a little in your pan; set them in a slow oven, and turn them every day whilst they be through y dry; so keep them for use.

You may dry pippens the same way, only as your turn them grate over them a little sugar.

376. *To preserve* CURRANS *in bunches*.

Boil your sugar to the fourth degree of boiling, tie your currans up in bunches, then place them in order in the sugar, and give them several covered boilings, skim them quick, and let them not have above two or three seethings, then skim them again, and set them into the stove in the preserving pan, the next day drain them, and dress them in bunches, strow them with sugar, and dry them in a stove or in the sun.

377. *To dry* APRICOCKS.

To a pound of apricocks put three quarter of a pound of sugar, pare and stone them, to a layer of fruit lie a layer of sugar, let them stand till the next day, then boil them again till they be clear, when cold take them out of the syrrup, and lay them upon glasses or china, and sift them over with double refined sugar, so set them on a stove to dry, next day if they be dry enough turn them and sift the other side with sugar; let the stones be broke and the kernels blanch'd, and give them a boil in the syrrup, then put them into the apricocks; you must not do too many at a time, for fear of breaking them in the syrrup; do a great many, and the more you do in it, the better they will taste.

378. *To make* JUMBALIS *another Way*.

Take a pound of meal dry, a pound of sugar finely beat, mix them together; then take the yolks of five or six eggs, as much thick cream as will make it up to a paste, and some corriander seeds; roll them and lay them on tins, prick and bake them in a quick oven; before you set them in the oven wet them with a little rose-water and double refin'd sugar, and it will ice them.

379. *To preserve* ORANGES *Whole*.

Take what quantity of oranges you have a mind to preserve, chip off the rind, the thiner and better, put them into water twenty-four hours, in that time shift them in the water (to take off the bitter) three times; you must shift them with boiling water, cold water makes them hard; put double the weight of sugar for oranges, dissolve your sugar in water, skim it, and clarify it with the white of an egg; before you put in your oranges, boil them in syrrup three or four times, three or four days betwixt each time; you must take out the inmeat of the oranges very clean, for fear of mudding the syrup.

380. *To make* JAM *of* DAMSINS.

Take damsins when they are ripe, and to two pounds of damsins take a pound of sugar, put your sugar into a pan with a jill of water, when you have boiled it put in your damsins, let them boil pretty quick, skim them all the time they are boiling, when your syrrup looks thick they are enough put them into your pots, and when they are cold cover them with a paper dip'd in brandy, tie them up close, and keep them for use.

381. *To make clear* Cakes *of* Gooseberries.

Take a pint of jelly, a pound and a quarter of sugar, make your jelly with three or four spoonfuls of water, and put your sugar and jelly together, set it over the fire to heat, but don't let it boil, then put it into the cake pots, and set it in a slow oven till iced over.

382. *To make* BULLIES CHEESE.

Take half a peck or a quartern of bullies, whether you please, pick off the stalks, put them in a pot, and stop them up very close, set them in a pot of water to boil for two hours, and be sure your pot be full of water, and boil them whilst they be enough, then put them in a hair-sieve to drain the liquor from the bullies; and to every quart of liquor put a pound and a quarter of sugar, boil it over a slow fire, keeping it stirring all the time: You may know when it is boiled high enough by the parting from the pan, and cover it with papers dip'd in brandy, so tie it up close, and keep it for use.

383. *To make* JAM *of* BULLIES.

Take the bullies that remained in the sieve, to every quart of it take a pound of sugar, and put it to your jam, boil it over a slow fire, put it in pots, and keep it for use.

384. *To make* SYRRUP *of* GILLIFLOWERS.

Take five pints of clipt gilliflowers, two pints of boiling water and put to them, then put them in an earthen pot to infuse a night and a day, take a strainer and strain them out; to a quart of your liquor put a pound and half of loaf sugar, boil it over a slow fire, and skim it whilst any skim rises; so when it is cold bottle it for use.

385. *To pickle* GILLIFLOWERS.

Take clove gilliflowers, when they are at full growth, clip them and put them into a pot, put them pretty sad down, and put to them some white wine vinegar, as much as will cover them; sweeten them with fine powder sugar, or common loaf; when you put in your sugar stir them up that your sugar may go down to the bottom; they must be very sweet; let them stand two or three days, and then put in a little more vinegar; so tie them up for use.

386. *To pickle* CUCUMBERS *sliced*.

Pare thirty large cucumbers, slice them into a pewter dish, take six onions, slice and strow on them some salt, so cover them and let them stand to drain twenty four hours; make your pickle of white wine vinegar, nutmeg, pepper, cloves and mace, boil the spices in the pickle, drain the liquor clean from the cucumbers, put them into a deep pot, pour the liquor upon them boiling hot, and cover them very close; when they are cold drain the liquor from them, give it another boil, and when it is cold pour it on them again; so keep them for use.

387. *To make* CUPID HEDGEHOG'S.

Take a quarter of a pound of jordan almonds, and half a pound of loaf sugar, put it into a pan with as much water as will just wet it, let it boil whilst it be so thick as will stick to your almonds, then put in your almonds and let them boil in it; have ready a quarter of a pound of small coloured comfits; take your almonds out of the syrrup one by one, and turn them round whilst they covered over, so lie them on a pewter dish as you do them, and set them before the fire, whilst you have done them all.

They are pretty to put in glasses, or to set in a desert.

388. *To make* ALMOND HEDGE-HOGS.

Take half a pound of the best almonds, and blanch them, beat them with two or three spoonfuls of rose-water in a marble-mortar very small, then take six eggs, (leave out two of the whites) beat your eggs very well, take half a pound of loaf sugar beaten, and four ounces of clarified butter, mix them all well together, put them into a pan, set them over the fire, and keep it stirring whilst it be stiff, then put it into a china-dish, and when it is cold put it up into the shape of an hedge hog, put currans for eyes, and a bit of candid orange for tongue; you may leave out part of the almonds unbeaten; take them and split them in two, then cut them in long bits to stick into your hedge hog all over, then rake two pints of cream custard to pour over your hedge hog, according to the bigness of your dish; lie round your dish edge slices of candid or preserved orange, which you have, so serve it up.

389. *To pot* SALMON *to keep half a Year*.

Take a side of fresh salmon, take out the bone, cut off the head and scald it; you must not wash it but wipe it with a dry cloth; cut it in three pieces, season it with mace, pepper, salt and nutmeg, put it into a flat pot with the skin side downward, lie over it a pound of butter, tie a paper over it, and send it to the oven, about an hour and a half will bake it; if you have more salmon in your pot than three pieces it will take more baking, and you must put in more butter; when it is baked take it out of your pot, and lie it on a dish plate to drain, and take off the skin, so season it over again, for if it be not well seasoned it will not keep; put it into your pot piece by piece; it will keep best in little pots, when you put it into your pots, press it well down with the back of your hand, and when it is cold cover it with clarified butter, and set it in a cool place; so keep it for use.

390. *To make a* CODDLIN PIE.

Take coddlins before they are over old, hang them over a slow fire to coddle, when they are soft peel off the skin, so put them into the water again, then cover 'em up with vine leaves, and let them hang over the fire whilst they be green; be sure you don't let them boil; lie them whole in the dish, and bake them in puff-paste, but leave no paste in the bottom of the dish; put to 'em a little shred lemon-peel, a spoonful of verjuice or juice of lemon, and as much sugar as you think proper, according to the largeness of your pie.

391. *To make a* COLLIFLOWER PUDDING.

Boil the flowers in milk, take the tops and lay then in a dish, then take three jills of cream, the yolks of eight eggs, and the whites of two, season it with nutmeg, cinnamon, mace, sugar, sack or orange-flower water, beat all well together, then pour it over the colliflower, put it into the oven, bake it as you would a custard, and grate sugar over it when it comes from the oven.

Take sugar, sack and butter for sauce.

392. *To make Stock for* HARTSHORN JELLY.

Take five or six ounces of hartshorn, put it into a gallon of water, hang it over a slow fire, cover it close, and let it boil three or four hours, so strain it; make it the day before you use it, and then you may have it ready for your jellies.

393. *To make* SYRRUP OF VIOLETS.

Take violets and pick them; to every pound of violets put a pint of water, when the water is just ready to boil put it to your violets, and stir them well together, let them infuse twenty four hours and strain them; to every pound of syrup, take almost two pounds of sugar, beat the sugar very well and put it into your syrrup, stir it that the sugar may dissolve, let it stand a day or two, stirring it two or three times, then set it on the fire, let be but warm and it will be thick enough.

You may make your syrrup either of violets or gilliflowers, only take the weight of sugar, let it stand on the fire till it be very hot, and the syrrup of violets must be only warm.

394. *To pickle* COCKLES.

Take cockles at a full moon and wash 'em, then put them in a pan, and cover them with a wet cloth, when they are enough put them into a stone bowl, take them out of the shells and wash them very well in their own pickle; let the pickle settle every time you wash them then clear it off; when you have cleaned 'em, put the pickle into a pan, with a spoonful or two of white wine and a little white wine vinegar, to you taste, put in a little Jamaica and whole pepper, boil it very well in the pickle, then put in you cockles, let 'em have a boil and skim 'em, when they are cold put them in a bottle with a little oil over them, set 'em in a cool place and keep 'em for use.

395. *To preserve Quinces whole or in quarters*.

Take the largest quinces when they are at full growth, pare them and throw them into water, when you have pared them cut them into quarters, and take out the cores; if you would have any whole you must take out the cores with a scope; save all the cores and parings, and put them in a pot or pan to coddle your quinces in, with as much water as will cover them, so put in your quinces in the middle of your paring into the pan, (be sure you cover them close up at the top) so let them hang over a slow fire whilst they be thoroughly tender, then take them out and weigh them; to every pound of quince take a pound of loaf sugar, and to every pound of sugar take a pint of the same water you coddled your quinces in, set your water and sugar over the fire, boil it and skim it, then put in your quinces, and cover it close up, set it over a slow fire, and let it boil whilst your quinces be red and the syrrup thick, then put them in pots for use, dipping a paper in brandy to lie over them.

396. *To pickle* SHRIMPS.

Take the largest shrimps you can get, pick them out of the shells, boil them in a jill of water, or as much water as will cover them according as you have a quantity of shrimps, strain them thro' a hair-sieve, then put to the liquor a little spice, mace, cloves, whole pepper, white wine, white wine vinegar, and a little salt to your taste; boil them very well together, when it is cold put in your shrimps, they are fit for use.

397. *To pickle* MUSCLES.

Wash your muscles, put them into a pan as you do your cockles, pick them out of the shells, and wash them in the liquor; be sure you take off the beards, so boil them in the liquor with spices, as you do your cockles, only put to them a little more vinegar than you do to cockles.

398. *To pickle* WALNUTS *green*.

Gather walnuts when they are as you can run a pin through them, pare them and put them in water, and let them lie four or five days, stirring it twice a day to take out the bitter, then put them in strong salt and water, let them lie a week or ten days, stirring it once or twice a day, then put them in fresh salt and water, and hang them over a fire, put to them a little allum, and cover them up close with vine leaves, let them hang over a slow fire whilst they be green, but be sure don't let them boil, when they are green pat them into a sieve to drain the water from them.

399. *To make* PICKLE *for them*.

Take a little good alegar, put to it a little long pepper and Jamaica pepper, a few bay leaves, a little horse-radish, a handful or two of mustard-seed, a little salt and a little rockambol if you have any, if not a few shalots; boil them altogether in the alegar, which put to your walnuts and let it stand three or four days, giving them a scald once a day, then tie them up for use.

A spoonful of this pickle is good for fish-sauce, or a calf's head ash.

400. *To pickle* WALNUTS *black*.

Gather walnuts when they are so tender that you can run a pin thro' them, prick them all with a pin very well, lie them in fresh water, and let them lie for a week, shifting them once a day; make for them a strong salt and water, and let them lie whilst they be yellow, stirring them once a day, then take 'em out of the salt and water, and boil it, put it on the top of your walnuts, and let your pot stand in the corner end, scald them once or twice a day whilst they be black.

You may make the same pickle for those, as you did for the green ones.

401. *To pickle* OYSTERS.

Take the largest oysters you can get, pick them whole out of the shell, and take off the beards, wash them very well in their own pickle, so let the pickle settle, and clear it off, put it into a stew-pan, put to it two or three spoonfuls of white wine, and a little white wine vinegar; don't put in any water, for if there be not pickle enough of their own get a little cockle-pickle and put to it, a little Jamaica pepper, white pepper and mace, boil and skim them very well; you must skim it before you put in your spices, then put in your oysters, and boil them in the pickle, when they are cold put them into a large bottle with a little oil on the top, set them in a cool place and keep them for use.

402. *To pickle large* CUCUMBERS.

Take cucumbers and put them in a strong salt and water, let them lie whilst they be throughly yellow, then scald them in the same salt and water they lie in, set them on the fire, and scald them once a day whilst they are green; take the best alegar you can get, put to it a little Jamaica pepper and black pepper, some horse-radish in slices, a few bay leaves, and a little dill and salt, so scald your cucumbers twice or thrice in this pickle; then put them up for use.

403. *To pickle* ONIONS.

Take the smallest onions you can get, peel and put them into a large quantity of fair water, let them lie two days and shift them twice a day; then drain them from the water, take a little distill'd vinegar, put to 'em two or three blades of mace, and a little white pepper and salt, boil it, and pour it upon your onions, let them stand three days, so put them into little glasses, and tie a bladder over them; they are very good done with alegar; for common use, only put in Jamaica pepper instead of mace.

404. *To pickle* ELDER BUDS.

Take elder buds when they are the bigness of small walnuts, lie them in a strong salt and water for ten days, and then scald them in fresh salt and water, put in a lump of allum, let them stand in the corner end close cover'd up, and scalded once a day whilst green.

You may do radish cods or brown buds the same way.

405. *To make the* Pickle.

Take a little alegar or white wine vinegar, and put to it two or three blades of mace, with a little whole pepper and Jamaica pepper, a few bay leaves and salt, put to your buds, and scald them two or three times, then they are fit for use.

406. *To pickle* MUSHROOMS.

Take mushrooms when fresh gather'd, sort the large ones from the buttons, cut off the stalks, wash them in water with a flannel, have a pan of water ready on the fire to boil 'em in, for the less they lie in the water the better; let them have two or three boils over the fire, then put them into a sieve, and when you have drained the water from them put them into a pot, throw over them a handful of salt, stop them up close with a cloth, and let them stand two or three hours on the hot hearth or range end, giving your pot a shake now and then; then drain the pickle from them, and lie them in a cloth for an hour or two, so put into them as much distill'd vinegar as will cover them, let them lie a week or ten days, then take them out, and put them in dry bottles; put to them a little white pepper, salt and ginger sliced, fill them up with distill'd vinegar, put over 'em a little sweet oil, and cork them up close; if your vinegar be good they will keep two or three years; I know it by experience.

You must be sure not to fill your bottles above three parts full, if you do they will not keep.

407. *To pickle* MUSHROOMS *another Way*.

Take mushrooms and wash them with a flannel, throw them into water as you wash them, only pick the small from the large, put them into a pot, throw over them a little salt, stop up your pot close with a cloth, boil them in a pot of water as you do currans when you make a jelly, give them a shake now and then; you may guess when they are enough by the quantity of liquor that comes from them; when you think they are enough strain from them the liquor, put in a little white wine vinegar, and boil it in a little mace, white pepper, Jamaica pepper, and slic'd ginger; then it is cold put it to the mushrooms, bottle 'em and keep 'em for use.

They will keep this way very well, and have more of the taste of mushrooms, but they will not be altogether so white.

408. *To pickle* POTATOE CRABS.

Gather your crabs when they are young, and about the bigness of a large cherry, lie them in a strong salt and water as you do other pickles, let them stand for a week or ten days, then scald them in the same water they lie in twice a day whilst green; make the same pickle for them as you do for cucumbers; be sure you scald them twice or thrice in the pickle and they will keep the better.

409. *To pickle large* BUTTONS.

Take your buttons, clean 'em and cut 'em in three or four pieces, put them into a large sauce-pan to stew in their own liquor, put to them a little Jamaica and whole pepper, a blade or two of mace, and a little salt, cover it up, let it stew over a slow fire whilst you think they are enough, then strain from them their liquor, and put to it a little white wine vinegar or alegar, which you please, give it a boil together, and when it is cold put it to your mushrooms, and keep them for use.

You may pickle flaps the same way.

410. *To make* CATCHUP.

Take large mushrooms when they are fresh gathered, cut off the dirty ends, break them small in your hands, put them in a stone-bowl with a handful or two of salt, and let them stand all night; if you don't get mushrooms enough at once, with a little salt they will keep a day or two whilst you get more, so put 'em in a stew-pot, and set them in an oven with household bread; when they are enough strain from 'em the liquor, and let it stand to settle, then boil it with a little mace, Jamaica and whole black pepper, two or three shalots, boil it over a slow fire for an hour, when it is boiled let it stand to settle, and when it is cold bottle it; if you boil it well it will keep a year or two; you must put in spices according to the quantity of your catchup; you must not wash them, nor put to them any water.

411. *To make* MANGO *of* CUCUMBERS *or* SMALL MELONS.

Gather cucumbers when they are green, cut a bit off the end and take out all the meat; lie them in a strong salt and water, let them lie for a week or ten days whilst they be yellow, then scald them in the same salt and water they lie in whilst green, then drain from them the water; take a little mustard-seed, a little horse-radish, some scraped and some shred fine, a handful of shalots, a claw or two of garlick if you like the taste, and a little shred mace; take six or eight cucumbers shred fine, mix them amongst the rest of the ingredients, then fill your melons or cucumbers with the meat, and put in the bits at the ends, tie them on with a string, so as will well cover them, and put into it a little Jamaica and whole pepper, a little horse-radish and a handful or two of mustard-seed, then boil it, and pour it upon your mango; let it stand in the corner end two or three days, scald them once a day, and then tie them up for use.

412. *To pickle* GARKINS.

Take garkins of the first growth, pick 'em clean, put 'em in a strong salt and water, let 'em lie a week or ten days whilst they be throughly yellow, then scald them in the same salt and water they lie in, scald them once a day, and let them lie whilst they are green, the set them in the corner end close cover'd.

413. *To make* PICKLE *for your* Cucumbers.

Take a little alegar, (the quantity must be equal to the quantity of your cucumbers, and so must your seasoning) a little pepper, a little Jamaica and long pepper, two or three shalots, a little horse-radish scraped or sliced, and little salt and a bit of allum, boil them altogether, and scald your cucumbers two or three times with your pickle, so tie them up for use.

414. *To pickle* COLLIFLOWER *white*.

Take the whitest colliflower you can get, break it in pieces the bigness of a mushroom; take as much distill'd vinegar as will cover it, and put to it a little white pepper, two or three blades of mace, and a little salt, then boil it and pour it on your colliflowers three times, let it be cold, then put it into your glasses or pots, and wet a bladder to tie over it to keep out the air.

415. *To pickle* Red Cabbage.

Take a red cabbage, chuse it a purple red, for the light red never proves a good colour; so take your cabbage and shred it in very thin slices, season it with pepper and salt very well, let it lie all night upon a broad tin, or a dripping-pan; take a little alegar, put to it a little Jamaica pepper, and two or three rases of ginger, boil them together, and when it is cold pour it upon your cabbage, and in two or three days time it will be fit for use.

You may throw a little colliflower among it, and it will turn red.

416. *To pickle* Colliflower *another Way*.

Take the colliflower and break it in pieces the bigness of a mushroom, but leave on a short stalk with the head; take some white wine vinegar, into a quart of vinegar, put six-pennyworth of cochineal beat well, also a little Jamaica and whole pepper, and a little salt, boil them in vinegar, pour it over the colliflower hot, and let it stand two or three days close covered up; you may scald it once in three days whilst it be red, when it is red take it out of pickle, and wash the cochineal off in the pickle, so strain it through a hair sieve, and let it stand a little to settle, then put it to your colliflower again, and tie it up for use; the longer it lies in the pickle the redder it will be.

417. *To pickle* WALNUTS *white*.

Take walnuts when they are at full growth and can thrust a pin through them, the largest sort you can get, pare them, and cut a bit off one end whilst you see the white, so you must pare off all the green, if you cut through the white to the kernel they will be spotted, and put them in water as you pare them; you must boil them in salt and water as you do mushrooms, and will take no more boiling than a mushroom; when they are boiled lay them on a dry cloth to drain out of the water, then put them into a pot, and put to them as much distill'd vinegar as will cover them, let them lie two or three days; then take a little more vinegar, put to it a few blades of mace, a little white pepper and salt, boil 'em together, when it is cold take your walnuts out of the other pickle and put into that, let them lie two or three days, pour it from them, give it another boil and skim it, when it is cold put to it your walnuts again, put them into a bottle, and put over them a little sweet oil, cork them up, and set them in a cool place; if your vinegar be good they will keep as long as the mushrooms.

418. *To pickle* BARBERRIES.

Take barberries when full ripe, put them into a pot, boil a strong salt and water, then pour it on them boiling hot.

419. *To make* BARLEY-SUGAR.

Boil barley in water, strain it through a hair-sieve, then put the decoction into clarified sugar brought to a candy height, or the last degree of boiling, then take it off the fire, and let the boiling settle, then pour it upon a marble stone rubb'd with the oil of olives, when it cools and begins to grow hard, cut it into pieces, and rub it into lengths as you please.

420. *To pickle* PURSLAIN.

Take the thickest stalks of purslain, lay them in salt and water six weeks, then take them out, put them into boiling water, and cover them well; let them hang over a slow fire till they be very green, when they are cold put them into pot, and cover them well with beer vinegar, and keep them covered close.

421. *To make* PUNCH *another Way.*

Take a quart or two of sherbet before you put in your brandy, and the whites of four or five eggs, beat them very well, and set it over the fire, let it have a boil, then put it into a jelly bag, so mix the rest of your acid and brandy together, (the quantity you design to make) heat it and run it all through your jelly bag, change it in the running off whilst it look fine; let the peel of one or two lemons lie in the bag; you may make it the day before you use it, and bottle it.

422. *To make new* COLLEGE PUDDINGS.

Grate an old penny loaf, put to it a like quantity of suet shred, a nutmeg grated, a little salt and some currans, then beat some eggs in a little sack and sugar, mix all together, and knead it as stiff as for manchet, and make it up in the form and size of a turkey's egg, but a little flatter; take a pound of butter, put it in a dish or stew-pan, and set it over a clear fire in a chafing-dish, and rub your butter about the dish till it is melted, then put your puddings in, and cover the dish, but often turn your puddings till they are brown alike, and when they are enough grate some sugar over them, and serve them up hot.

For a side-dish you must let the paste lie for a quarter of an hour before you make up your puddings.

423. *To make a* CUSTARD PUDDING.

Take a pint of cream, mix it with six eggs well beat, two spoonfuls of flour, half a nutmeg grated, a little salt and sugar to your taste; butter your cloth, put it in when the pan boils, baste it just half an hour, and melt butter for the sauce.

424. *To make* FRYED TOASTS.

Chip a manchet very well, and cut it round ways in toasts, then take cream and eight eggs seasoned with sack, sugar, and nutmeg, and let these toasts steep in it about an hour, then fry them in sweet butter, serve them up with plain melted butter, or with butter, sack and sugar as you please.

425. *To make* SAUCE *for* Fish or Flesh.

Take a quart of vinegar or alegar, put it into a jug, then take Jamaica pepper whole, some sliced ginger and mace; a few cloves, some lemon-peel, horse radish sliced, sweet herbs, six shalots peeled, eight anchovies, and two or three spoonfuls of shred capers, put all those in a linen bag, and put the bag into your alegar or vinegar, stop the jug close, and keep it for use.

A spoonful cold is an addition to sauce for either fish or flesh.

426. *To make a* savoury Dish of VEAL.

Cut large collops of a leg of veal, spread them abroad on a dresser, hack them with the back of a knife, and dip them in the yolks of eggs, season them with nutmeg, mace, pepper and salt, then make forc'd-meat with some of your veal, beef-suit, oysters chop'd, and sweet herbs shred fine, and the above spice, strow all these over your collops, roll and tie them up, put them on skewers, tie them to a spit and roast them; and to the rest of your forc'd-meat add the yolk of an egg or two, and make it up in balls and fry them, put them in a dish with your meat when roasted, put a little water in the dish under them, and when they are enough put to it an anchovy, a little gravy, a spoonful of white wine, and thicken it up with a little flour and butter, so fry your balls and lie round the dish, and serve it up.

This is proper for a side-dish either at noon or night.

427. *To make* FRENCH BREAD.

Take half a peck of fine flour, the yolks of six eggs and four whites, a little salt, a pint of ale yeast, and as much new milk made warm as will make it a thin light paste, stir it about with your hand, but be sure you don't knead them; have ready six wooden quarts or pint dishes, fill them with the paste, (not over full) let them stand a quarter of an hour to rise, then turn them out into the oven, and when they are baked rasp them. The oven must be quick.

428. *To make* GINGER-BREAD *another Way.*

Take three pounds of fine flour, and the rind of a lemon dried and beaten to powder, half a pound of sugar, or more if you like it, a little butter, and an ounce and a half of beaten ginger, mix all these together and wet it pretty stiff with nothing but treacle; make it into rolls or cakes which you please; if you please you may add candid orange peel and citron; butter your paper to bake it on, and let it be baked hard.

429. *To make* QUINCE CREAM.

Take quinces when they are full ripe, cut them in quarters, scald them till they be soft, pare them, and mash the clear part of them, and the pulp, and put it through a sieve, take an equal weight of quince and double refin'd sugar beaten and sifted; and the whites of eggs beat till it is as white as snow, then put it into dishes.

You may do apple cream the same way.

430. *To make* CREAM *of any preserved Fruit.*

Take half a pound of the pulp of any preserved fruit, put it in a large pan, put to it the whites of two or three eggs, beat them well together for an hour, then with a spoon take off, and lay it heaped up high on the dish and salver without cream, or put it in the middle bason.

Rasberries will not do this way.

431. *To dry* PEARS *or* PIPPENS *without Sugar.*

Take pears or apples and wipe them clean, take a bodkin and run it in at the head, and out at the stalk, put them in a flat earthen pot and bake them, but not too much; you must put a quart of strong new ale to half a peck of pears, tie twice papers over the pots that they are baked in, let them stand till cold then drain them, squeeze the pears flat, and the apples, the eye to the stalk, and lay 'em on sieves with wide holes to dry, either in a stove or an oven not too hot.

432. *To preserve* MULBERRIES *whole.*

Set some mulberries over the fire in a skellet or preserving pan, draw from them a pint of juice when it is strain'd; then take three pounds of sugar beaten very fine, wet the sugar with the pint of juice, boil up your sugar and skim it, put in two pounds of ripe mulberries, and let them stand in the syrrup till they are throughly warm, then set them on the fire, and let them boil very gently; do them but half enough, so put them by in the syrrup till next day, then boil them gently again; when the syrrup is pretty thick and well stand in round drops when it is cold, they are enough, so put all in a gally-pot for use.

433. *To make* ORANGE CAKES.

Cut your oranges, pick out the meat and juice free from the strings and seeds, set it by, then boil it, and shift the water till your peels are tender, dry them with a cloth, mince them small, and put them to the juice; to a pound of that weigh a pound and a half of double refin'd sugar; dip your lumps of sugar in water, and boil it to a candy height, take it off the fire and put in your juice and peel, stir it well, when it is almost cold put it into a bason, and set it in a stove, then lay it thin on earthen plates to dry, and as it candies fashion it with a knife, and lay them on glasses; when your plate is empty, put more out of your bason.

434. *To dry* APRICOCKS *like* PRUNELLOS.

Take a pound of apricocks before they be full ripe, cut them in halves or quarters, let them boil till they be very tender in a thin syrup, and let them stand a day or two in the stove, then take them out of the syrrup, lay them to dry till they be as dry as prunellos, then box 'em, if you please you may pare them.

You may make your syrrup red with the juice of red plumbs.

435. *To preserve great white* PLUMBS.

To a pound of white plumbs take three quarters of a pound of double refin'd sugar in lumps, dip your sugar in water, boil and skim it very well, slit your plumbs down the seam; and put them into the syrrup with the slit downwards; let them stew over the fire a quarter of an hour, skim them very well, then take them off, and when cold cover them up; turn them in the syrrup two or three times a day for four or five days, then put them into pots and keep them for use.

436. *To make* Gooseberry Wine *another Way.*

Take gooseberries when they are full ripe, pick and beat them in a marble mortar; to every quart of berries put a quart of water, and put them into a tub and let them stand all night, then strain them through a hair-sieve, and press them very well with your hand; to every gallon of juice put three pounds of four-penny sugar; when your sugar is melted put it into the barrel, and to as many gallons of juice as you have, take as many pounds of Malaga raisins, chop them in a bowl, and put them in the barrel with the wine; be sure let not your barrel be over full, so close it up, let it stand three months in the barrel, and when it is fine bottle it, but not before.

437. *To pickle* NASTURTIUM BUDS.

Gather your little nobs quickly after the blossoms are off, put them in cold water and salt three days, shifting them once a day; then make a pickle for them (but don't boil them at all) of some white wine, and some white wine vinegar, shalot, horse-radish, whole pepper and salt, and a blade or two of mace; then put in your seeds, and stop 'em close up. They are to be eaten as capers.

438. *To make* ELDER-FLOWER WINE.

Take three or four handfuls of dry'd elder-flowers, and ten gallons of spring water, boil the water, and pour in scalding hot upon the flowers, the next day put to every gallon of water five pounds of Malaga raisins, the stalks being first pick'd off, but not wash'd, chop them grosly with a chopping knife, then put them into your boiled water, stir the water, raisins and flowers well together, and do so twice a day for twelve days, then press out the juice clear as long as you can get any liquor; put it into a barrel fit for it, stop it up two or three days till it works, and in a few days stop it up close, and let it stand two or three months, then bottle it.

439. *To make* PEARL BARLEY PUDDING.

Take half a pound of pearl barley, cree it in soft water, and shift it once or twice in the boiling till it be soft; take five eggs, put to them a pint of good cream, and half a pound of powder sugar, grate in half a nutmeg, a little salt, a spoonful or two of rose-water, and half a pound of clarified butter; when your barley is cold mix them altogether, so bake it with a puff-paste round your dish-edge.

Serve it up with a little rose-water, sugar and butter for your sauce.

440. *To make* Gooseberry Vinegar *another Way.*

Take gooseberries when they are full ripe, bruise them in a marble mortar or wooden bowl, and to every upheap'd half peck of berries take a gallon of water, put it to them in the barrel, let it stand in a warm place for two weeks, put a paper on the top of your barrel, then draw it off, wash out the barrel, put it in again, and to every gallon add a pound of coarse sugar; set it in a warm place by the fire, and let it stand whilst christmas.

441. *To preserve* APRICOCKS *green.*

Take apricocks when they are young and tender, coddle them a little, rub them with a coarse cloth to take off the skin, and throw them into water as you do them, and put them in the same water they were coddled in, cover them with vine leaves, a white paper, or something more at the top, the closer you keep them the sooner they are green; be sure you don't let them boil; when they are green weigh them, and to every pound of apricocks take a pound of loaf sugar, put it into a pan, and to every pound of sugar a jill of water, boil your sugar and water a little, and skim it, then put in your apricocks, let them boil together whilst your apricocks look clear, and your syrrup thick, skim it all the time it is boiling, and put them into a pot covered with a paper dip'd in brandy.

442. *To make* ORANGE CHIPS *another Way.*

Pare your oranges, not over thin but narrow, throw the rinds into fair water as you pare them off, then boil them therein very fast till they be tender, filling up the pan with boiling water as it wastes away, then make a thin syrrup with part of the water they are boiled in, put in the rinds, and just let them boil, then take them off, and let them lie in the syrrup three or four days, then boil them again till you find the syrrup begin to draw between your fingers, take them off from the fire and let them drain thro' your cullinder, take out but a few at a time, because if they cool too fast it will be difficult to get the syrrup from them, which must be done by passing every piece of peel through your fingers, and lying them single on a sieve with the rind uppermost, the sieve may be set in a stove, or before the fire; but in summer the sun is hot enough to dry them.

Three quarters of a pound of sugar will make syrrup to do the peels of twenty-five oranges.

443. *To make* MUSHROOM POWDER.

Take about half a peck of large buttons or slaps, clean them and set them in an earthen dish or dripping pan one by one, let them stand in a slow oven to dry whilst they will beat to powder, and when they are powdered sift them through a sieve; take half a quarter of a ounce of mace, and a nutmeg, beat them very fine, and mix them with your mushroom powder, then put it into a bottle, and it will be fit for use.

You must not wash your mushrooms.

444. *To preserve* APRICOCKS *another Way.*

Take your apricocks before they are full ripe, pare them and stone them, and to every pound of apricocks take a pound of lump loaf sugar, put it into your pan with as much water as will wet it; to four pounds of sugar take the whites of two eggs beat them well to a froth, mix them well with your sugar whilst it be cold, then set it over the fire and let it have a boil, take it off the fire, and put in a spoonful or two of water, then take off the skim, and do so three or four times whilst any skim rises, then put in your apricocks, and let them have a quick boil over the fire, then take them off and turn them over, let them stand a little while covered, and then set them on again, let them have another boil and skim them, then take them out one by one; set on your syrrup again to boil down, and skim it, then put in your apricocks again, and let them boil whilst they look clear, put them in pots, when they are cold cover them over with a paper dipt in brandy, and tie another paper at the top, set them in a cool place, and keep them for use.

445. *To pickle* MUSHROOMS *another Way.*

When you have cleaned your mushrooms put them into a pot, and throw over them a handful of salt, and stop them very close with a cloth, and set them in a pan of water to boil about an hour, give them a shake now and then in the boiling, then take them out and drain the liquor from them, wipe them dry with a cloth, and put them up either in white wine vinegar or distill'd vinegar, with spices, and put a little oil on the top.

They don't look so white this way, but they have more the taste of mushrooms.

446. *How to fry* MUSHROOMS.

Take the largest and freshest flaps you can get, skin them and take out the gills, boil them in a little salt and water, then wipe them dry with a cloth; take two eggs and beat them very well, half a spoonful of wheat-flour, and a little pepper and salt, then dip in your mushrooms and fry them in butter.

They are proper to lie about stew'd mushrooms or any made dish.

447. *How to make an* ALE POSSET.

Take a quart of good milk, set it on the fire to boil, put in a handful or two of breadcrumbs, grate in a little nutmeg, and sweeten it to your taste; take three jills of ale and give it a boil; take the yolks of four eggs, beat them very well, then put to them a little of your ale, and mix all your ale and eggs together; then set it on the fire to heat, keep stirring it all the time, but don't let it boil, if you do it will curdle; then put it into your dish, heat the milk and put it in by degrees; so serve it up.

You may make it of any sort of made wine; make it half an hour before you use it, and keep it hot before the fire.

448. *To make* MINC'D PIES *another Way.*

Take half a pound of Jordan almonds, blanch and beat them with a little rosewater, but not over small; take a pound of beef-suet shred very fine, half a pound of apples shred small, a pound of currans well cleaned, half a pound of powder sugar, a little mace shred fine, about a quarter of a pound of candid orange cut in small pieces, a spoonful or two of brandy, and a little salt, so mix them well together, and bake it in a puff-paste.

449. *To make* SACK POSSET *another Way.*

Take a quart of good cream, and boil it with a blade or two of mace, put in about a quarter of a pound of fine powder sugar; take a pint of sack or better, set it over the fire to heat, but don't let it boil, then grate in a little nutmeg, and about a quarter of a pound of powder sugar; take nine eggs, (leave out six of the whites and strains) beat 'em very well, then put to them a little of your sack mix the sack and eggs very well together, then put to 'em the rest of your sack, stir it all the time you are pouring it in, set it over a slow fire to thicken, and stir it till it be as thick as custard; be sure you don't let it boil, if you do it will curdle, then pour it into your dish or bason; take your cream boiling hot, and pour to your sack by degrees, stirring it all the time you are pouring it in, then set it on a hot-hearth-stone; you must make it half an hour before you use it; before you set on the hearth cover it close with a pewter dish.

To make a FROTH *for them.*

Take a pint of the thickest cream you can get, and beat the whites of two eggs very well together, take off the cream by spoonfuls, and lie it in a sieve to drain; when you dish up the posset lie over it the froth.

450. *To dry* CHERRIES *another Way.*

Take cherries when full ripe, stone them, and break 'em as little as you can in the stoning; to six pounds of cherries take three pounds of loaf sugar, beat it, lie one part of your sugar under your cherries, and the other at the top, let them stand all night, then put them into your pan, and boil them pretty quick whilst your cherries change and look clear, then let them stand in the syrrup all night, pour the syrrup from them, and put them into a pretty large sieve, and set them either in the sun or before the fire; let them stand to dry a little, then lay them on white papers one by one, let them stand in the sun whilst they be thoroughly dry, in the drying turn them over, then put them into a little box; betwixt every layer of cherries lie a paper, and so do till all are in, then lie a paper at the top, and keep them for use.

You must not boil them over long in the syrrup, for if it be over thick it will keep them from drying; you may boil two or three pounds more cherries in the syrrup after.

451. *How to order* STURGEON.

If your sturgeon be alive, keep it a night and a day before you use it; then cut off the head and tail, split it down the back, and cut it into as many pieces as you please; salt it with bay salt and common salt, as you would do beef for hanging, and let it lie 24 hours; then tie it up very tight, and boil it in salt and water whilst it is tender; (you must not boil it over much) when it is boiled throw over it a little salt, and set it by till it be cold. Take the head and split it in two and tye it up very tight; you must boil it by itself, not so much as you did the rest, but salt it after the same manner.

452. *To make the* PICKLE.

Take a gallon of soft water, and make it into a strong brine; take a gallon of stale beer, and a gallon of the best vinegar, and let it boil together, with a few spices; when it is cold put in your sturgeon; you may keep it (if close covered) three or four months before you need to renew the pickle.

453. *To make* HOTCH-POTCH.

Take five or six pounds of fresh beef, put it in a kettle with six quarts of soft water, and an onion; set it on a slow fire, and let it boil til your beef is almost enough; then put in the scrag of a neck of mutton, and let them boil together till the broth be very good; put in two or three handfuls of breadcrumbs, two or three carrots and turnips cut small, (but boil the carrots in water before you put them in, else they will give your broth a taste) with half a peck of shill'd pease, but take up the meat before you put them in, when you put in the pease take the other part of your mutton and cut it in chops, (for it will take no more boiling than the pease) and put it in with a few sweet herbs shred very small, and salt to your taste.

You must send up the mutton chops in the dish with the hotch-potch.

When there are no pease to be had, you may put in the heads of asparagus, and if there be neither of these to be had, you may shred in a green savoy cabbage.

This is a proper dish instead of soop.

454. *To make* MINC'D COLLOPS.

Take two or three pounds of any tender parts of beef, (according as you would have the dish in bigness) cut it small as you would do minc'd veal; take an onion, shred it small, and fry it a light brown, in butter seasoned with nutmeg, pepper and salt, and put it into your pan with your onion, and fry it a little whilst it be a light brown; then put to it a jill of good gravy, and a spoonful of walnut pickle, or a little catchup; put in a few shred capers or mushrooms, thicken it up with a little flour and butter; if you please you may put in a little juice of lemon; when you dish it up, garnish your dish with pickle; and a few forc'd-meat-balls.

It is proper for either side-dish or top-dish.

455. *To make white* Scotch Collops *another Way.*

Take two pounds of the solid part of a leg of veal, cut it in pretty thin slices, and season it with a little shred mace and salt, put it into your stew-pan with a lump of butter, set it over the fire, keep it stirring all the time, but don't let it boil; when you are going to dish up the collops, put to them the yolks of two or three eggs, three spoonfuls of cream, a spoonful or two of white wine, and a little juice of lemon, shake it over the fire whilst it be so thick that the sauce sticks to the meat, be sure you don't let it boil.

Garnish your dish with lemon and sippets, and serve it up hot.

This is proper for either side-dish or top-dish, noon or night.

456. *To make* VINEGAR *another Way.*

Take as many gallons of water as you please, and to every gallon of water put in a pound of four-penny sugar, boil it for half an hour and skim it all the time; when it is about blood warm put to it about three or four spoonfuls of light yeast, let it work in the tub a night and a day, put it into your vessel, close up the top with a paper, and set it as near the fire as you have convenience, and in two or three days it will be good vinegar.

457. *To preserve* QUINCES *another Way.*

Take quinces, pare and put them into water, save all the parings and cores, let 'em lie in the water with the quinces, set them over the fire with the parings and cores to coddle, cover them close up at the top with the parings, and lie over them either a dishcover or pewter dish, and cover them close; let them hang over a very slow fire whilst they be tender; but don't let them boil; when they are soft take them out of the water, and weigh your quinces, and to every pound put a pint of the same water they were coddled in (when strained) and put to your quinces, and to every pound of quinces put a pound of sugar; put them into a pot or pewter flagon, the pewter makes them a much better colour; close them up with a little coarse paste, and set them in a bread oven all night; if the syrrup be too thin boil it down, put it to your quinces, and keep it for use.

You may either do it with powder sugar or loaf sugar.

458. *To make* Almond Cheesecakes *another Way*.

Take the peel of two or three lemons pared thick, boil them pretty soft, and change the water two or three times in the boiling; when they are boiled beat them very fine with a little loaf sugar, then take eight eggs, (leaving out six of the whites) half a pound of loaf or powder sugar, beat the eggs and sugar for half an hour, or better; take a quarter of a pound of the best almonds, blanch and beat them with three or four spoonfuls of rose-water, but not over small; take ten ounces of fresh butter, melt it without water, and clear off from it the butter-milk, then mix them altogether very well, and bake them in a slow oven in a puff-paste; before you put them into the tins, put in the juice of half a lemon.

When you put them in the oven grate over them a little loaf sugar.

You may make them without almonds, if you please.

You may make a pudding of the same, only leave out the almonds.

FINIS.

English Housewifry *improved*;

OR,

A SUPPLEMENT TO MOXON'S COOKERY.

CONTAINING,

Upwards of Sixty Modern and Valuable RECEIPTS IN
   PASTRY MADE DISHES

PRESERVING MADE WINES, &c. &c.

Collected by a PERSON of JUDGMENT.

SUPPLEMENT TO MOXON'S Cookery.

1. *A* GRANADE.

Take the caul of a leg of veal, lie it into a round pot; put a layer of the flitch part of bacon at the bottom, then a layer of forc'd-meat, and a layer of the leg part of veal cut as for collops, 'till the pot is fill'd up; which done, take the part of the caul that lies over the edge of the pot, close it up, tie a paper over, and send it to the oven; when baked, turn it out into your dish.—*Sauce.* A good light-brown gravy, with a few mushrooms, morels, or truffles; serve it up hot.

2. *The fine Brown* JELLY.

Boil four calf's feet in six quarts of water 'till it is reduced to three pints, tale off the feet and let the stock cool, then melt it, and have ready in a stew-pan, a spoonful of butter hot, add to it a spoonful of fine flour, stir it with a wood spoon over a stove-fire, 'till it is very brown, but not burnt, then put the jelly out, and let it boil; when cold take off the fat, melt the jelly again and put to it half a pint of red port, the juice and peel of half a lemon, white pepper, mace, a little Jamaica pepper, and a little salt; then have ready the whites of four eggs, well froth'd, and put them into the jelly, (take care the jelly be not too hot when the whites are put in) stir it well together, and boil it over a quick fire one minute, run it thro' a flannel bag and turn it back till it is clear, and what form you would have it, have that ready, pour a little of the jelly in the bottom, it will soon starken; then place what you please in it, either pigeon or small chicken, sweet-bread larded, or pickled smelt or trout, place them in order, and pour on the remainder of the jelly. You may send it up in this form, or turn it into another dish, with holding it over hot water; but not till it is thoroughly hardened.

3. *To make a* MELLON.

Make the leanest forc'd-meat that you can, green it as near the colour of mellon as possible with the juice of spinage, as little of the juice as you can; put several herbs in it, especially parsley, shred fine, for that will help to green it; roll it an inch and a half thick, lay one half in a large mellon mould, well buttered and flowered, with the other half the full size of the mould, sides and all; then put into it as many stew'd oysters as near fills it with liquor sufficient to keep them moist, and close the forc'd-meat well together; close the melon and boil it till you think it is enough; then make a small hole (if possible not to be perceived) pour in a little more of the liquor that the oysters were stew'd in hot, and serve it up with hot sauce in the dish. It must be boiled in a cloth, and is either for a first or second course.

4. *Hot* CHICKEN PIE.

Order the chickens as for fricassy, and form the pie deep, lay in the bottom a mince-meat made of the chicken's livers, ham, parsley and yolks of eggs; season with white pepper, mace, and a little salt; moisten with butter, then lay the chicken above the minc'd meat, and a little more butter; cover the pie and bake it two hours; when baked take off the fat, and add to it white gravy, with a little juice of lemon. Serve this up hot.

5. SHEEP'S RUMPS *with* Rice.

Stew the rumps very tender, then take 'em out to cool, dip them in egg and bread-crumbs, and fry them a light brown; have ready half a pound of rice, well wash'd and pick'd, and half a pound of butter; let it stew ten minutes in a little pot; then add a pint of good gravy to the rice and butter, and let it stew half an hour longer; have ready six onions boil'd very tender, and six yolks of boil'd eggs, stick them with cloves; then place the sheep rumps on the dish, and put round them the rice as neatly as you can; place the onions and eggs over the rice, so serve it up hot.

6. SHEEP'S TONGUES *broil'd*.

The tongues being boil'd, put a lump of butter in a stew-pan, with parsley and green onions cut small; then split the tongues, but do not part them, and put them in the pan, season them with pepper, herbs, mace, and nutmeg; set them a moment on the fire, and strow crumbs of bread on them; let them be broil'd and dish them up, with a high gravy sauce.

7. *To lard* OYSTERS.

Make a strong essence of ham and veal, with a little mace; then lard the large oysters with a fine larding pin; put them, with as much essence as will cover them, into a stew-pan; let them stew and hour, or more, over a slow fire. They are used for garnishing, but when you make a dish of them, squeeze in a Seville orange.

8. VEAL COULEY.

Take a little lean bacon and veal, onion, and the yellow part of a carrot, put it into a stew-pan; set it over a slow fire, and let it simmer till the gravy is quite brown, then put in small gravy, or boiling water; boil it a quarter of an hour, and then it is ready for use. Take two necks of mutton, bone them, lard one with bacon, the other with parsley; when larded, put a little couley over a slow stove, with a slice of lemon whilst the mutton is set, then skewer it up like a couple of rabbits, put it on the spit and roast it as you would any other mutton; then serve it up with ragoo'd cucumbers. This will do for first course; bottom dish.

9. *The* MOCK TURTLE.

Take a fine large calf's head, cleans'd well and stew'd very tender, a leg of veal twelve pounds weight, leave out three pounds of the finest part of it; then take three fine large fowls, (bone them, but leave the meat as whole as possible,) and four pounds of the finest ham sliced; then boil the veal, fowls bones, and the ham in six quarts of water, till it is reduced to two quarts, put in the fowl and the three pounds of veal, and let them boil half an hour; take it off the fire and strain the gravy from it; add to the gravy three pints of the best white wine, boil it up and thicken it; then put in the calf's-head; have in readiness twelve large forc'd-meat-balls, as large as an egg, and twelve yolks of eggs boil'd hard. Dish it up hot in a terreen.

10. *To dress* OX LIPS.

Take three or four ox lips, boil them as tender as possible, dress them clean the day before they are used; then make a rich forc'd-meat of chicken or half-roasted rabbits, and stuff the lips with it; they will naturally turn round; tie them up with pack-thread and put them into gravy to stew; they must stew while the forc'd-meat be enough. Serve them up with truffles, morels, mushrooms, cockscombs, forc'd-meat balls, and a little lemon to your taste.

This is a top-dish for second, or side dish for first course.

11. *To make* POVERADE.

Take a pint of good gravy, half a jill of elder vinegar, six shalots, a little pepper and salt, boil all these together a few minutes, and strain it off. This is a proper sauce for turkey, or any other sort of white fowls.

12. *To pot* PARTRIDGES.

Take the partridges and season them well with mace, salt and a little pepper; lie 'em in the pot with the breast downwards, to every partridge put three quarters of a pound of butter, send them to the oven, when baked, drain them from the butter and gravy, and add a little more seasoning, then put them close in the pot with the breasts upwards, and when cold, cover them well with the butter, suit the pot to the number of the partridges to have it full. You may pot any sort of moor game the same way.

13. *To pot* PARTRIDGES *another Way.*

Put a little thyme and parsley in the inside of the partridges, season them with mace, pepper and salt; put them in the pot, and cover them with butter; when baked, take out the partridges, and pick all the meat from the bones, lie the meat in a pot (without beating) skim all the butter from the gravy, and cover the pot well with the butter.

14. *To pot* CHARE.

Scrape and gut them, wash and dry them clean, season them with pepper, salt, mace, and nutmeg; let the two last seasonings be higher than the other; put a little butter at the bottom of the pot, then lie in the dish, and put butter at the top, three pounds of butter to four pounds of chare; when they are baked (before they are cold) pour off the gravy and butter, put two or three spoonfuls of butter into the pot you keep them in, then lie in the dish, scum the butter clean from the gravy, and put the butter over the dish, so keep it for use.

15. SALMON *en* Maigre.

Cut some slices of fresh salmon the thickness of your thumb, put them in a stew-pan with a little onion, white pepper and mace, and a bunch of sweet herbs, pour over it half a pint of white wine, half a jill of water, and four ounces of butter (to a pound and half of salmon;) cover the stew-pot close, and stew it half an hour; then take out the salmon, and place it on the dish; strain off the liquor, and have ready craw-fish, pick'd from the shell, or lobster cut in small pieces; pound the shells of the craw-fish, or the seeds of the lobster, and give it a turn in the liquor; thicken it, and serve it up hot with the craw-fish, or lobster, over the salmon.

Trouts may be done the same way, only cut off their heads.

16. LOBSTER A'L'ITALIENNE.

Cut the tail of the lobster in square pieces, take the meat out of the claws, bruise the red part of the lobster very fine, stir it in a pan with a little butter, put some gravy to it; strain it off while hot, then put in the lobster with a little salt; make it hot, and send it up with sippets round your dish.

17. *To do* CHICKENS, *or any* FOWL'S FEET.

Scald the feet till the skin will come off, then cut off the nails; stew them in a pot close cover'd set in water, and some pieces of fat meat till they are very tender; when you set them on the fire, put to them some whole pepper, onion, salt, and some sweet herbs; when they are taken out, wet them over with the yolk of an egg, and dridge them well with bread-crumbs; so fry them crisp.

18. LARKS *done in* JELLY.

Boil a knuckle of veal in a gallon of water till it is reduced to three pints, (it must not be covered but done over a clear fire) scum it well and clarify it, then season the larks with pepper and salt, put them in a pot with butter, and send them to the oven; when baked take them out of the butter whilst hot, take the jelly and season it to your taste with pepper and salt; then put the jelly and larks into a pan together, and give them a scald over the fire; so lie them in pots and cover them well with jelly. When you use them, turn them out of the pots, and serve them up.

19. *The Fine* CATCHUP.

Take three quarts of red port, a pint of vinegar, one pound of anchovies unwash'd, pickle and altogether, half an ounce of mace, ten cloves, eight races of ginger, one spoonful of black pepper, eight ounces of horseradish, half a lemon-peel, a bunch of winter-savory, and four shalots; stew these in a pot, within a kettle of water, one full hour, then strain it thro' a close sieve, and when it is cold bottle it; shake it well before you bottle it, that the sediment may mix. You may stew all the ingredients over again, in a quart of wine for present use.

20. WALNUT CATCHUP.

Take the walnuts when they are ready for pickling, beat them in a mortar, and strain the juice thro' a flannel bag; put to a quart of juice a jill of white wine, a jill of vinegar, twelve shalots sliced, a quarter of an ounce of mace, two nutmegs sliced, one ounce of black pepper, twenty four cloves, and the peels of two Seville oranges, pared so thin that no white appears, boil it over a slow fire very well, and scum it as it boils; let it stand a week or ten days cover'd very close, then pour it thro' the bag, and bottle it.

21. *A very good* White *or* Almond Soop.

Take veal, fowl, or any white meat, boiled down with a little mace, (or other spice to your taste) let these boil to mash, then strain off the gravy; take some of the white fleshy part of the meat and rub it thro' a cullender; have ready two ounces of almonds beat fine, rub these thro' the cullender, then put all into the gravy, set it on the fire to thicken a little, and stir in it two or three spoonfuls of cream, and a little butter work'd in flour; then have ready a French roll crisp'd for the middle, and slips of bread cut long like Savoy biskets. Serve it up hot.

22. ALMOND PUDDING.

Take one pound of almonds, blanch'd and beat fine, one pint of cream, the yolks of twelve eggs, two ounces of grated bread, half a pound of suet, marrow, or melted butter, three quarters of a pound of fine sugar, a little lemon-peel and cinnamon; bake it in a slow oven, in a dish, or little tins. The above are very good put in skins.

23. ALMOND PUDDING *another Way*.

Boil a quart of cream, when cold, mix in the whites of seven eggs well beat; blanch five ounces of almonds, beat them with rose or orange-flower water, mix in the eggs and cream; sweeten it to your taste with fine powder sugar, then mix in a little citron or orange, put a thin paste at the bottom, and a thicker round the edge of the dish. Bake in a slow oven.—Sauce. Wine and sugar.

24. Almond Cheesecakes *another Way*.

Six ounces of almonds, blanch'd and beat with rose-water; six ounces of butter beat to cream; half a pound of fine sugar; six eggs well beat, and a little mace. Bake these in little tins, in cold butter paste.

25. *A* LEMON PUDDING *another Way*.

Take a quarter of a pound of almonds, three quarters of a pound of sugar, beat and searc'd, half a pound of butter; beat the almonds with a little rose-water, grate the rinds of two lemons, beat eleven eggs, leave out two whites, melt the butter an stir it in; when the oven is ready mix all these well together, with the juice of one or two lemons to your taste; put a thin paste at the bottom, and a thicker round the edge of the dish.

Sauce. Wine and sugar.

26. POTATOE PUDDING *another Way*.

Take three quarters of a pound of potatoes, when boil'd and peel'd, beat them in a mortar with a quarter of a pound of suet or butter, (if butter, melt it) a quarter of a pound of powder sugar, five eggs well beat, a pint of good milk, one spoonful of flour, a little mace or cinnamon, and three spoonfuls of wine or brandy; mix all these well together, and bake it in a pretty quick oven.

Sauce. Wine and butter.

27. CARROT PUDDING *another Way*.

Take half a pound of carrots, when boil'd and peel'd, beat them in a mortar, two ounces of grated bread, a pint of cream, half a pound of suet or marrow, a glass of sack, a little cinnamon, half a pound of sugar, six eggs well beat, leaving out three of the whites, and a quarter of a pound of macaroons; mix all well together; puff-paste round the dish-edge.

Sauce. Wine and sugar.

28. WHITE POTT *another Way*.

A layer of white bread cut thin at the bottom of the dish, a layer of apples cut thin, a layer of marrow or suet, currans, raisins, sugar and nutmeg, then the bread, and so on, as above, till the dish is fill'd up; beat four eggs, and mix them with a pint of good milk, a little sugar and nutmeg, and pour it over the top. This should be made three or four hours before it is baked.

Sauce. Wine and butter.

29. HUNTING PUDDING *another Way*.

Take a pound of grated bread, a pound of suet and a pound of currans, eight eggs, a glass of brandy, a little sugar, and a little beat cinnamon; mix these well together, and boil it two hours at the least.

30. ALMOND BISKETS.

Blanch a pound of almonds, lie them in water for three or four hours, dry them with a cloth, and beat them fine with eight spoonfuls of rose or orange-flower water; then boil a pound of fine sugar to wire-height, and stir in the almonds, mix them well over the fire; but do not let them boil; pour them into a bason, and beat them with a spoon 'till quite cold; then beat six whites of eggs, a quarter of a pound of starch, beat and searc'd, beat the eggs and starch together, 'till thick; stir in the almonds, and put them in queen-cake tins, half full, dust them over with a little searc'd sugar; bake 'em in a slow oven, and keep them dry.

31. *To make* ALMOND BUTTER

another Way.

Take a quart of cream, six eggs well beat, mix them and strain them into a pan, keep it stirring on the fire whilst it be ready to boil; then add a jack of sack, keeping it stirring till it comes to a curd; wrap it close in a cloth till the whey be run from it; then put the curd into a mortar, and beat it very fine, together with a quarter of a pound of blanch'd almonds, beaten with rose-water, and half a pound of loaf sugar; When all these are well beaten together, put it into glasses.

This will keep a fortnight.

32. APRICOCK JUMBALLS.

Take ripe apricocks, pare, stone, and beat them small, then boil them till they are thick, and the moisture dry'd up, then take them off the fire, and beat them up with searc'd sugar, to make them into pretty stiff paste, roll them, without sugar, the thickness of a straw; make them up in little knots in what form you please; dry them in a stove or in the sun. You may make jumballs of any sort of fruit the same way.

33. BURNT CREAM.

Boil a stick of cinnamon in a pint of cream, four eggs well beat, leaving out two whites, boil the cream and thicken it with the eggs as for a custard; then put it in your dish, and put over it half a pound of loaf sugar beat and searc'd; heat a fire-shovel red-hot, and hold it over the top till the sugar be brown. So serve it up.

34. *Little* PLUMB CAKES.

Take two pounds of flour dry'd, three pounds of currans well wash'd, pick'd and dry'd, four eggs beaten with two spoonfuls of sack, half a jack of cream, and one spoonful of orange-flower or rose-water; two nutmegs grated, one pound of butter wash'd in rose-water and rub'd into the flour, and one pound of loaf sugar searc'd, mix all well together, and put in the currans; butter the tins and bake them in a quick oven; half an hour will bake it.

35. York GINGER-BREAD *another Way.*

Take two pounds and a half of stale bread grated fine, (but not dry'd) two pound of fine powder sugar, an ounce of cinnamon, half an ounce of mace, half an ounce of ginger, a quarter of an ounce of saunders, and a quarter of a pound of almonds; boil the sugar, saunders, ginger, and mace in half a pint of red wine; then put in three spoonfuls of brandy, cinnamon, and a quarter of an ounce of cloves; stir in half the bread on the fire, but do not let it boil; pour it out, and work in the rest of the bread with the almonds; then smother it close half an hour; print it with cinnamon and sugar search'd, and keep it dry.

36. GINGER-BREAD *in little Tins.*

To three quarters of a pound of flour, put half a pound of treacle, one pound of sugar, and a quarter of a pound of butter; mace, cloves, and nutmeg, in all a quarter of an ounce; a little ginger, and a few carraway seeds; melt the butter in a glass of brandy, mix altogether with one egg; then butter the tins, and bake them in a pretty quick oven.

37. OAT-MEAL CAKES.

Take a peck of fine flour, half a peck of oat-meal, and mix it well together; put to it seven eggs well beat, three quarts of new milk, a little warm water, a pint of sack, and a pint of new yeast; mix all these well together, and let it stand to rise; then bake them. Butter the stone every time you lie on the cakes, and make them rather thicker than a pancake.

38. BATH CAKES.

Take two pounds of flour, a pound of sugar, and a pound of butter; wash the butter in orange-flower water, and dry the flour; rub the butter into the flour as for puff-paste, beat three eggs fine in three spoonfuls of cream, and a little mace and salt, mix these well together with your hand, and make them into little cakes; rub them over with white of egg, and grate sugar upon them; a quarter of an hour will bake them in a slow oven.

39. *A Rich White* PLUMB-CAKE.

Take four pounds of flour dry'd, two pounds of butter, one pound and a half of double refin'd sugar beat and searc'd, beat the butter to cream, then put in the sugar and beat it well together; sixteen eggs leaving out four yolks; a pint of new yeast; five jills of good cream, and one ounce of mace shred; beat the eggs well and mix them with the butter and sugar; put the mace in the flour; warm the cream, mix it with the yeast, and run it thro' a hair sieve, mix all these into a paste; then add one pound of almonds blanch'd and cut small, and six pounds of currans well wash'd, pick'd and dry'd; when the oven is ready, stir in the currans, with one pound of citron, lemon or orange; then butter the hoop and put it in.

This cake will require two hours and a half baking in a quick oven.

40. *An* ISING *for the* CAKE.

One pound and a half of double-refin'd sugar, beat and searc'd; the whites of four eggs, the bigness of a walnut of gum-dragon, steep'd in rose or orange-flower water; two ounces of starch, beat fine with a little powder-blue (which adds to the whiteness) while the cake is baking beat the ising and lie it on with a knife as soon as the cake is brought from the oven.

41. LEMON BRANDY.

Pour a gallon of brandy into an earthen pot, put to it the yellow peel of two dozen lemons, let it stand two days and two nights, then pour two quarts of spring water into a pan and dissolve in it two pounds of refin'd loaf sugar, boil it a quarter of an hour, and put it to the brandy; then boil and scum three jills of blue milk, and mix all together, let it stand two days more, then run it thro' a flannel bag, or a paper within a tunnel, and bottle it.

42. *To make* RATIFEE *another Way.*

Take a hundred apricocks stones, break them, and bruise the kernels, then put them in a quart of the best brandy; let them stand a fortnight; shake them every day; put to them six ounces of white sugar-candy, and let them stand a week longer; then put the liquor thro' a jelly bag, and bottle it for use.

43. *To preserve* GRAPES *all Winter.*

Pull them when dry, dip the stalks about an an inch of boiling water, and seal the end with wax; chop wheat straw and put a little at the bottom of the barrel, then a layer of grapes, and a layer of straw, 'till the barrel is fill'd up; do not lie the bunches too near one another; stop the barrel close, and set it in a dry place; but not any way in the sun.

44. *To preserve* GRAPES *another Way.*

Take ripe grapes and stone them; to every pound of grapes take a pound of double-refined sugar; let them stand till the sugar is dissolved; boil them pretty quick till clear; then strain out the grapes, and add half a pound of pippen jelly, and half a pound more sugar; boil and skim it till a jelly; put in the grapes to heat; afterwards strain them out, and give the jelly a boil; put it to the grapes and stir it till near cold; then glass it.

45. BARBERRY CAKES.

Draw off the juice as for curran jelly, take the weight of the jelly in sugar, boil the sugar to sugar again; then put in the jelly, and keep stirring till the sugar is dissolved; let it be hot, but not boil; then pour it out, and stir it three or four times; when it is near cold drop it on glasses in little cakes, and set them in the stove. If you would have them in the form of jumballs, boil the sugar to a high candy, but not to sugar again, and pour it on a pie plate; when it will part from the plate cut it, and turn them into what form you please.

46. BARBERRY DROPS.

When the barberries are full ripe, pull 'em off the stalk, put them in a pot, and boil them in a pan of water till they are soft, then pulp them thro' a hair-sieve, beat and searce the sugar, and mix as much of the searc'd sugar with the pulp, as will make it of the consistance of a light paste; then drop them with a pen-knife on paper (glaz'd with a slight stone) and set them within the air of the fire for an hour, then take them off the paper and keep them dry.

47. *To candy* ORANGES *whole another Way.*

Take the Seville oranges, pare off the red as thin as you can, then tie them in a thin cloth (with a lead weight to keep the cloth down) put 'em in a lead or cistern of river water, let them lie five or six days, stirring 'em about every day, then boil them while they are very tender, that you may put a straw thro' them; mark them at the top with a thimble, cut it out, and take out all the inside very carefully, then wash the skins clean in warm water, and set them to drain with the tops downwards; fine the sugar very well, and when it is cold put in the oranges; drain the syrrup from the oranges, and boil it every day till it be very thick, then once a month; one orange will take a pound of sugar.

48. *To candy* GINGER.

Take the thickest races of ginger, put them in an earthen pot, and cover them with river water; put fresh water to them every day for a fortnight; then tie the ginger in a cloth, and boil it an hour in a large pan of water; scrape off the brown rind, and cut the inside of the races as broad and thin as you can, one pound of ginger will take three pounds of loaf sugar; beat and searce the sugar, and put a layer of the thin-slic'd ginger, and a layer of searc'd sugar into an earthen bowl, having sugar at the top; stir it well every other day for a fortnight, then boil it over a little charcoal; when it is candy-height take it out of the pan as quick as you can with a spoon, and lie it in cakes on a board; when near cold take them off and keep them dry.

49. *To preserve* WINE-SOURS.

Take wine-sours and loaf sugar an equal weight, wet the sugar with water; the white of one egg will fine four pounds of sugar, and as the scum rises throw on a little water; then take off the pan, let it stand a little to settle and skim it; boil it again while any scum rises; when it is clear and a thick syrrup, take it off, and let it stand till near cold; then nick the plumbs down the seam, and let them have a gentle heat over the fire; take the plumbs and syrrup and let them stand a day or two, but don't cover them; then give them another gentle heat; let them stand a day longer, and heat them again; take the plumbs out and drain them, boil the syrrup and skim it well, then put the syrrup on the wine-sours, and when cold, put them into bottles or pots, tie a bladder close over the top, so keep them for use.

50. CURRAN JELLY.

Take eight pounds of ripe, pick'd fruit, put these into three pounds of sugar boil'd candy height, and so let these simmer till the jelly will set; then run it off clear thro' a flannel bag, and glass it up for use. This never looks blue, nor skims half so much, as the other way.

51. *To preserve red or white* CURRANS *whole.*

Pick two pounds of currans from the stalks, then take a pound and a half of loaf sugar, and wet it in half a pint of curran juice, put in the berries, and boil them over a slow fire till they are clear; when cold put them in small berry bottles, with a little mutton suet over them.

52. SYRRUP OF POPPIES.

Take two pounds of poppy flowers, two ounces of raisins, shred them, and to every pound of poppies put a quart of boiling water, half an ounce of sliced liquorice, and a quarter of an ounce of anniseeds; let these stand twelve hours to infuse, then strain off the liquor, and put it upon the same quantity of poppies, raisins, liquorice, and anniseeds as before, and let this stand twelve hours to infuse, which must be in a pitcher, set within a pot or pan of hot water; then strain it, and take the weight in sugar, and boil it to a syrrup: when it is cold, bottle it.

53. *To make* BLACK PAPER *for drawing Patterns.*

Take a quarter of a pound of mutton suet, and one ounce of bees wax, melt both together and put in as much lamp black as will colour it dark enough, then spread it over your paper with a rag, and hold it to the fire to make it smooth.

54. GOOSEBERRY VINEGAR *another Way.*

To every gallon of water, put six pounds of ripe gooseberries; boil the water and let it be cold, squeeze the berries, and then pour on the water; let it stand cover'd three days pretty warm to work, stirring it once a day; then strain it off, and to every six gallons put three pounds of coarse sugar, let it stand till it has done working, then bung it up, and keep it moderately warm, in nine months it will be ready for use.

55. *To make bad Ale into good strong Beer.*

Draw off the ale into a clean vessel,

(supposing half a hogshead) only leave out eight or ten quarts, to which put four pounds of good hops, boil this near an hour; when quite cold, put the ale and hops into the hogshead, with eight pounds of treacle, mix'd well with four or five quarts of boil'd ale; stir it well together, and bung it up close: Let it stand six months, then bottle it for use.

56. *Green* GOOSEBERRY WINE.

To every quart of gooseberries, take a quart of spring water, bruise them in a mortar, put the water to them and let them stand two or three days, then strain it off, and to every gallon of liquor put three pounds and a half of sugar, then put it into the barrel, and it will of itself rise to a froth, which take off, and keep the barrel full; when the froth is all work'd off, bung it up for six weeks, then rack it off, and when the lees are clean taken out, put the wine into the same barrel; and to every gallon put half a pound of sugar, made in syrrup, and when cold mix with wine; to every five gallons, have an ounce of isinglass, dissolv'd in a little of the wine, and put in with the syrrup, so bung it up; when fine, you may either bottle it or draw it out of the vessel. Lisbon sugar is thought the best. This wine drinks like sack.

57. GINGER WINE.

Take fourteen quarts of water, three pounds of loaf sugar, and one ounce of ginger sliced thin, boil these together half an hour, fine it with the whites of two eggs; when new milk warm put in three lemons, a quart of brandy, and a white bread toast, covered on both sides with yeast; put all these together into a stand, and work it in one day; then tun it: It will be ready to bottle in five days, and be ready to drink in a week after it is bottled.

58. COWSLIP WINE *another Way*.

To five gallons of water, put two pecks of cowslip peeps, and thirteen pounds of loaf sugar; boil the sugar and water with the rinds of two lemons, half an hour, and fine it with the whites of two eggs; when it is near cold put in the cowslips, and set on six spoonfuls of new yeast, work it two days, stirring it twice a day; when you squeeze out the peeps to tun it, put in the juice of six lemons, and when it has done working in the vessel, put in the quarter of an ounce of isinglass, dissolv'd in the little of the wine till it is a jelly; add a pint of brandy, bung it close up two months, then bottle it. This is right good.

59. STRONG MEAD *another Way*.

To thirty quarts of water, put ten quarts of honey, let the water be pretty warm, then break in the honey, stirring it till it be all dissolv'd, boil it a full half hour, when clean scum'd that no more will rise, put in half an ounce of hops, pick'd clean from the stalks; a quarter of an ounce of ginger sliced (only put in half the ginger) and boil it a quarter of an hour longer; then lade it out into the stand thro' a hair-tems, and put the remainder of the ginger in, when it is cold tun it into the vessel, which must be full; but not clay'd up till near a month: make it the latter end of *September*, and keep it a year in the vessel after it is clay'd up.

60. FRENCH BREAD.

To half a peck of flour, put a full jill of new yeast, and a little salt, make it with new milk (warmer than from the cow) first put the flour and barm together, then pour in the milk, make it a little stiffer than a seed-cake, dust it and your hands well with flour, pull it in little pieces, and mould it with flour very quick; put it in the dishes, and cover them with a warm cloth (if the weather requires it) and let them rise till they are half up, then set them in the oven, (not in the dishes, but turn them with tops down upon the peel;) when baked rasp them.

61. *The fine* RUSH CHEESE.

Take one quart of cream, and put to it a gallon of new milk, pretty warm, adding a good spoonful of earning; stir in a little salt, and set it before the fire till it be cum'd; then put it into a vat in a cloth; after a day and night turn it out of the vat into a rush box nine inches in length and five in breadth. The rushes must be wash'd every time the cheese is turn'd.

FINIS.

A BILL of FARE FOR EVERY SEASON of the YEAR.

For *JANUARY*.
First Course.
At the Top Gravy Soop.
Remove Fish.
At the Bottom a Ham.
In the Middle stew'd Oysters or Brawn.
For the four corners.
A Fricassy of Rabbits, Scotch Collops, boil'd Chickens, Calf Foot
Pie, or Oyster Loaves.
Second Course.
At the Top Wild Ducks.
At the Bottom a Turkey.
In the Middle Jellies or Lemon Posset.
For the four Corners.
Lobster and Tarts, Cream Curds, stew'd Pears or preserv'd Quinces.
For *FEBRUARY*.
First Course.
At the Top a Soop remove.
At the Bottom Salmon or stew'd Breast of Veal.
For the four Corners.
A Couple of Fowls with Oyster Sauce, Pudding, Mutton Cutlets, a
Fricassy of Pig's Ears.
Second Course.
At the Top Partridges.
At the Bottom a Couple of Ducks.
For the four Corners.
Stew'd Apples, preserv'd Quinces, Custards, Almond Cheese Cakes.
In the Middle Jellies.
For *MARCH*.
First Course.
At the Top a boil'd Turkey, with Oyster Sauce.
At the bottom a Couple of roast Tongues or roast Beef.
In the Middle Pickles.
Two Side-dishes, a Pigeon Pie and Calf Head Hash.
For the four Corners.
Stew'd Crab or Oysters, Hunters Pudding, a brown Fricassy, stew'd
Eels, or broil'd Whitings.
Second Course.
At the Top Woodcocks or wild Ducks.
At the Bottom Pig or Hare.
In the Middle Jellies or Sweetmeats.
For the four Corners.

Raspberry Cream, Tarts, stew'd Apples, and preserv'd Apricocks.

For *APRIL*.
First Course.
At the Top stew'd Fillet of Veal.
At the Bottom a roast Leg of Mutton.
Two Side-dishes, Salt Fish and Beef-Steaks.
In the Middle a Hunters Pudding.
Second Course.
At the Top roast Chickens and Asparagus.
At the Bottom Ducks.
In the Middle preserv'd Oranges.
For the four Corners.
Damasin Pie, Cream Curds, Lobster, and cold Pot.

For *MAY*.
First Course.
At the Top stew'd Carp or Tench.
At the Bottom a stew'd Rump of Beef.
In the Middle a Sallet.
For the four Corners
A Fricassy of Tripes, boil'd Chickens, a Pudding, Olives of Veal.
Second Course.
At the Top Rabbits or Turkey Pouts.
At the Bottom green Goose or young Ducks.
For the four Corners.
Lemon Cream, Quince Cream, Tarts, Almond Custards.
In the Middle Jellies.

For *JUNE*.
First Course.
At the Top roast Pike.
At the Bottom Scotch Collops.
In the Middle stew'd Crab.
For the four Corners.
Boil'd Chickens, Quaking Pudding, roast Tongue, with Venison Sauce, Beans and Bacon.
Second Course.
At the Top a Turkey.
At the Bottom Ducks or Rabbits.
In the Middle Strawberries.
Two Side dishes, roast Lobster and Pease.
For the four Corners.
Green Codlings, Apricock Custard, Sweetmeat Tarts, preserv'd Damsins, or Flummery.

For *JULY*.
First Course.

At the Top green Pease Soop, remove stew'd Breast of Veal white.
At the Bottom a Haunch of Venison.
In the Middle a Pudding.
Two Side-dishes, a Dish of Fish, and a Fricassy of Rabbits.
Second Course.
At the Top Partridges or Pheasants.
At the Bottom Ducks or Turkey.
In the Middle a Dish of Fruit.
For the four Corners.
Solomon Gundie, Lobster, Tarts, Chocolate Cream.

For *AUGUST*.
First Course.
At the Top Fish.
At the Bottom Venison Pasty.
In the Middle Herb Dumplings.
For the four Corners.
Fricassy of Rabbits, stew'd Pigeons, boil'd Chickens, Fricassy of Veal Sweetbreads with Artichoke Bottoms.
Second Course.
At the Top Pheasants or Partridges.
At the Bottom wild Ducks or Teal.
In the Middle Jellies or Syllabubs.
For the four Corners.
Preserv'd Apricocks, Almond Cheese-cakes, Custards, and Sturgeon.

For *SEPTEMBER*.
First Course.
At the Top collar'd Calf Head, with stew'd Pallets and Veal Sweetbreads, and forc'd Meat-Balls.
At the Bottom Udder and Tongue or a Haunch of Venison
In the Middle an Ambler of Cockles, or roast Lobster.
Two Side dishes, Pigeon Pie and boiled Chickens.
Second Course.
At the Top a roast Pheasant.
At the Bottom a Turkey.
For the four Corners.
Partridges, Artichoke-Bottoms fry'd, Oyster Loaves, and Teal.

For *OCTOBER*.
First Course.
At the Top stew'd Tench and Cod's Head.
At the Bottom roast Pork or a Goose.
Two Side-dishes, roast Fish, and boil'd Fowl and Bacon.

For the four Corners.
Jugg'd Pigeons, Mutton Collops, Beef Rolls, and Veal Sweetbreads fricassy'd.
In the Middle minc'd Pies or Oyster Loaves.
Second Course.
At the Top Wild Fowl.
At the Bottom a Hare.
In the Middle Jellies.
Two Side-dishes, roasted Lobster and fry'd Cream.
For the four Corners.
Preserv'd Quinces, or stew'd Pears, Sturgeon, cold Tongue, and Orange Cheese Cakes.

For *NOVEMBER*.
First Course.
At the Top a Dish of Fish.
At the Bottom a Turkey Pie.
Two Side-dishes, Scotch Collops, and boil'd Tongue with Sprouts.
In the Middle scallop'd Oysters.
Second Course.
At the Top a Dish of Wild Fowl.
At the Bottom roast Lobster.
In the Middle Lemon Cream.
For the four Corners.
Tarts, Curds, Apricocks, and Solomon Gundie.

For *DECEMBER*.
First Course.
At the Bottom boil'd Fowls.
Two Side dishes, Bacon and Greens, and a Dish of Scotch Collops.
In the Middle minc'd Pies or Pudding.
Second Course.
At the Top a Turkey.
In the Middle hot Apple Pie.
For the four Corners.
Custard, Raspberry Cream, cold Pot and Crabs.

A SUPPER

For *JANUARY*.
At the Top a Dish of Plumb Gruel. Remove, boil'd Fowls.
At the Bottom a Dish of Scotch Collops.
In the Middle Jellies.
For the four Corners.
Lobster, Solomon-Gundie, Custard, Tarts.

For *FEBRUARY*.

At the Top a Dish of Fish.
Remove, a Couple of roasted Fowls.
At the Bottom wild Ducks.
For the four Corners.
Collar'd Pig, Cheese Cakes, stew'd Apples and Curds.
In the Middle hot minc'd Pies.
For *MARCH*.
At the Top a Sack Posset.
Remove, a Couple of Ducks.
At the Bottom a boil'd Turkey, with Oyster Sauce.
In the Middle Lemon Posset.
Two Side-dishes, roasted Lobster, Oyster Pie.
For the four Corners.
Almond Custards, Flummery, Cheese-Cakes, and stew'd Apples.
For *APRIL*.
At the Top boiled Chickens.
At the Bottom a Breast of Veal.
In the Middle Jellies.
For the four Corners.
Orange Pudding, Custards, Tarts, and stew'd Oysters.
For *MAY*.
At the Top a Dish of Fish.
At the Bottom Lamb Steaks or Mutton.
In the Middle Lemon Cream or Jellies.
Two Side-dishes, Tarts, Raspberry Cream.
For the four Corners.
Veal sweetbreads, stew'd Spinage, with potched Eggs and Bacon,
Oysters in scallop'd Shells, boiled Chickens.
For *JUNE*.
At the Top boil'd Chickens.
At the Bottom a Tongue.
In the Middle Lemon Posset.
For the four Corners.
Cream Curds or Custards, potted Ducks, Tarts, Lobsters, Artichokes or Pease.
For *JULY*.
At the Top Scotch Collops.
At the Bottom roast Chickens.
In the Middle stew'd Mushrooms.
For the four Corners.
Custards, Lobsters, split Tongue, and Solomon Gundie.
For *AUGUST*.
At the Top stewed Breast of Veal.

At the Bottom roast Turkey.
In the Middle Pickles or Fruit.
For the four Corners.
Cheese Cakes and Flummery, preserved Apricocks, preserved Quinces.
For *SEPTEMBER*.
At the Top boil'd Chickens.
At the Bottom a carbonated Breast of Mutton, with Caper Sauce.
In the Middle Oysters in scallop Shells, or stew'd Oysters.
Two Side Dishes, hot Apple Pie and Custard.
For *OCTOBER*.
At the Top Rice Gruel.
Remove, a Couple of Ducks.
At the Bottom a boil'd Turkey with Oyster Sauce.
In the Middle Jellies.
For the four Corners.
Lobster or Crab, Black Caps, Custard or Cream, Tarts or collar'd Pig.
For *NOVEMBER*.
At the Top Fish.
At the Bottom Ducks or Teal.
In the Middle Oyster Loaves.
Remove, a Dish of Fruit.
Two Side Dishes, minc'd Pies, Mutton Steaks, with Mushrooms and Balls.
For *DECEMBER*.
At the Top boil'd Chickens.
At the Bottom a Dish of Scotch Collops or Veal Cutlets.
In the Middle Brawn.
Remove, Tarts.
For the four Corners.
Boil'd Whitings or fry'd Soles, new College Puddings, Tullouy Sausages, Scotch Custard.
[Illustration: *A SUPPER in SUMMER*.
1
2 3
4 5 6
7 8
9
1. Boil'd Chickens. 2. Preserv'd Oranges or Apricocks. 3. Flummery. 4. Asparagus. 5. Lemon Posset. 6. Roast Lobster. 7. Stew'd Apples. 8. Almond Cheese Cakes. 9. Lamb.]
[Illustration: *A DINNER in SUMMER*.
1
2 3 4

5
1. Cod's Head or Salmon. 2. Boil'd Chickens. 3. A fine Pudding or roasted Lobster. 4. Beans and Bacon. 5. Stew'd Breast of Veal.]
[Illustration: SECOND COURSE.
1
2 3
4
5 6
7
1. Two young Turkeys or Ducklings. 2. Stew'd Apples. 3. Custards. 4. Jellies or Lemon Posset. 5. Tarts. 6. Preserv'd Oysters. 7. Green Geese or young Rabbits.]
[Illustration: *A DINNER in WINTER*.
1
2 3
4
5 6
7
1. A Soop. 2. Scotch Collops. 3. Boil'd Chickens. 4. Stew'd Oysters or roasted Lobster. 5. A Hunters Pudding. 6. Roasted Tongue. 7. A Ham or roast Beef. Remove. 1 Fish.]
[Illustration: SECOND COURSE
1
2 3
4 5 6
7 8
9
1. A Turkey. 2. Almond Cheese-cakes. 3. Sturgeon. 4. Partridges. 5. Jellies. 6. A Hare or Woodcocks. 7. Collar'd Cream. 8. Cream Curds. 9. Ducks or Pig.]
[Illustration: *A SUPPER in WINTER*.
1
2 3
4
5 6
7
1. Gruel or Sack Posset. 2. Tarts. 3. Lobster. 4. Jellies or Lemon Cream. 5. Solomon Gundie. 6. Custards. 7. Boil'd Turkey with Oyster Sauce. Remove. 1. Wild Duck.]
[Illustration: *A DINNER in SUMMER*.
1
2 3

4 5 6
7 8 9
10 11 12
13 14
15

1. Craw Fish Soop.
2. Moor Game.
3. A Granade.
4. Apples stew'd green.
5. Boil'd Partridge.
6. Cherries.
7. Stew'd Sweetbreads, and Pallets.
8. Jellies or Pine-apples.
9. Roast Teal.
10. Apricocks.
11. Artichokes.
12. Sweet-meat Tarts.
13. Fry'd Soals.
14. Turkey Pout roasted and larded.
15. A Haunch of Venison.]

[Illustration: *A* GRAND TABLE in *WINTER*.

1
2 3 4
5 6 7 8
9 10 11 12 13
14 15 16 17
18 19 20
21

1. Vermicelly Soop. 2. Sweet Patties. 3. A Fricassy of Beast Patties. 4. Stew'd Crab. 5. Olives of Veal. 6. Preserv'd Damsins. 7. Preserv'd Oranges. 8. Marinaded Pigeons. 9. A boil'd Turkey with Oyster Sauce. 10. Cream Curds. 11. A Pyramid of dry'd Sweetmeats. 12. Flummery. 13. A Ham. 14. A white Fricassy of Chickens. 15. Preserv'd Apricocks. 16. Preserv'd Quinces. 17. A brown Fricassy of Rabbits. 18. A Fricassy of Veal Sweetmeats. 19. Minc'd Pies. 20. Oyster Loaves. 21. Haunce of Venison, or Roast Beef. Remove. 1. Carp with Pheasant. Remove. 2. Grapes. Remove. 3. Collar'd Beef. Remove. 4. Cheese-Cakes. Remove. 5. Quails. Remove. 8. Teal. Remove. 9. Two roasted Lobsters. Remove. 13. Woodcocks or Partridges. Remove. 14. Artichokes or young Peas. Remove. 17. Snipes. Remove. 18. Tarts. Remove. 19. Collar'd Pig. Remove. 20. Fruit. Remove. 21. Wild Ducks.]